LESSONS I LEARNED IN THE PROMISED LAND

By Jane Wheeler

Published By: Ray of Sunshine Ministries

Printed in the United States of America
First Printing: March 2020
Ray of Sunshine Ministries
ISBN:978-0-9958647-8-8 Paperback
ISBN:978-0-9958647-9-5 ebook

Cataloguing Data Available From Library and Archives Canada

Scripture quotations are taken from The Holy Bible,
New International Version © 1973,1978,1984
By International Bible Society
Used by Permission from Zondervan Publishing House

Cover design: Jane Wheeler

Visit my website at www.rayofsunshineministries.com

Dedication & Scripture Meditation

This book is lovingly dedicated to the one who knows me so much more than I know myself, Almighty God, My Abba Father, His Son: Yeshua and the Holy Spirit.

Cover Design: Birds on Boat in the Sea of Galilee

Matthew 10:29-31 New International Version (NIV)
"Are not two sparrows sold for a penny? Yet not one of them will fall to the ground outside your Father's care. And even the very hairs of your head are all numbered. So don't be afraid; you are worth more than many sparrows."

Other Books By Jane Wheeler

It Is Finished "Tetelestai": The Most Powerful Words Ever Spoken
Free To Fly
Midweek Moments 2016 Blog Posts of Jane Wheeler
Midweek Moments 2017 Blog Posts of Jane Wheeler
The Complete Love Circle

Table of Contents

Introduction

I did not want to go to Israel, in fact I argued with God when He told me He wanted me to go, I was going to Scotland. I had decided in my heart that my next trip would be England, Scotland and Ireland, but alas, my way was not the way that won in the end.

Now, knowing what I know, would I have changed it and gone to Scotland instead? Not on your life! Israel met more than my wildest imaginations ever could have imagined.

It all began when I heard a song that haunted my brain, it played continuously in my mind at all hours of the day and night. It was called *"Fire of Your Spirit"* by Sarah Liberman. I watched the music video and scenes played out in historical and clear definition of the tent of the tabernacle exactly described in the Old Testament of the Bible. For a Bible teacher such as myself, I was astounded that someone was giving me a physical view of the tabernacle as described in the book of Leviticus.

I could not stop watching it and seeing the setup of everything listed in the Bible from how the tent should be set up, how the priests should prepare to enter the tent, ceremonial washing and what should be placed inside.

I was in awe of the landscape around the tent, I thought it would be all sand, as I pictured deserts to be, but in the video it was "rocky" and upon going to Israel, I found that "rocky" was the landscape the tent would have been set upon.

The song pulled me in, and I could not figure out why. The song was in Hebrew and I could not speak Hebrew, but after listening to the song over and over, I could almost sing along with it.

I could not figure out what was going on.....I was so captivated by this song.

It has almost been a year since I was in Israel and this book has remained stuck on my computer for most of this time. The trip changed my life, it was mind blowing, it was more than I could have ever imagined. It was not that I did not wish to publish my story, more it was fear of man and the fact that I could not answer the questions: "why me?" "is this true?" "I don't believe it."

I cannot blame anyone for those questions because I could not and still cannot answer them myself, so I sealed up the hope of sharing my experiences. That is until God convicted me, this month, of being selfish, afraid and not sharing the gifts He had shown me, more scared of the questions of man then the consequences of disobeying God.

God has showed me the results of someone this week who was suffering the consequences of not being obedient and it was not pretty, and I became convicted to obey.

I share this journey with you because I want to be "obedient". I realize only now as I write it that the events, the stories and the messages downloaded to me are in answer to my original prayer: I want the God of the extravagant.

He showed up!

CHAPTER 1

'Why' I Went to Israel

I discovered the song by accident. I was looking for Jewish music on the internet and I found several musicians dubbed as Messianic Jews. The music was lively, catchy and usually in Hebrew. Several musicians were listed, I knew none of them except Paul Wilbur and only because my friend had introduced me to his music, and I had seen him perform in the states.

Fielding off of his website were names like Joshua Aaron, Sarah Liberman, Marty Goetz, Karen Davis, Johnathan Settel, Ted Pearce. Being naïve of any of them I started looking at their various websites.

I came across Sarah Liberman's, *Fire of Your Spirit* song and was totally blown away.

Finally, someone put onto the screen, a picture of the Old Testament tabernacle tent. The video showed the priest preparing to enter the tent, the ceremonial washing, blowing of the shofar, the sprinkling of the animal blood with hyssop branches just like it was described in the Bible. The video moved inside the tent, along with the minora, the manna, the arc of the covenant, and the veil which separated the holy place from the holy of holies. This video was speaking my language even if it was in Hebrew!

I was enticed, drawn in and this song would not stop playing in my mind, day or night, it began to become "weird" after a week, really strange after a month and downright peculiar by a month and a half. I could almost talk Hebrew because I knew the words.

I started to pray about why this song was haunting my mind. I got no answers, so I started to look online at Sarah's website. I came across a website she was on that offered *Ascend 10 Day Program,* they called it an encounter with God.

I read about the Ascend course, looked at a couple of videos and the FAQs section knowing a trip to Israel was not in the works because I was going to Scotland. Yes, Scotland had been on my bucket list for some time.

The song would not leave my mind and after a month and a half I questioned if I was supposed to apply to the course. I started to fill out the application and there were some questions you had to really think about. It took about an hour and I was almost completed when the application disappeared off my computer screen. I took that to mean that I was wrong, and I was not supposed to fill out the application because I certainly was not going to Israel. Case was settled, Scotland it was!

After about another three weeks, I keep sensing the statement, "you have not applied yet" circulating around and around in my mind. I knew what it was referring to.

I re-opened the application and started applying all over again. This time it did not disappear and as I pushed send, little did I know I had sealed my fate about Scotland.

I got an answer back relatively quickly stating that the next phase for applying to the Ascend 10 Day Program was a phone interview which would happen near the end of January 2019, about four weeks away. I was given a time and date and waited.

The day of my phone interview, we were going to try Whatsapp so we could have a visual interview and actually see each other. I had figured out the time difference and to my surprise I had the time wrong. Instead of being at home waiting for the call, I was at a trade show, a wedding show, setting up our booth and hauling in items from the car.

It was so loud in the hall where we were setting up, I could not hear. I lost the call about three times and ran out to the car to see if I could hear clearer. The back trunk of the car was open and refused to shut just as a big diesel pickup truck pulled up behind me.

"I am so sorry, I cannot hear anything you are saying, let me go close the trunk!" I yelled as they were attempting to hear me and me them. The trunk decided at that moment to have an attitude problem and would not close.

"I am so sorry!" I repeated over and over.

I jumped back into the car and lost the call again; the service was not great in this area. I turned the key, shoved the car in gear and peeled out of the area I was in and drove to the front of the building where it would be quieter. I pushed redial and waited; apparently, I had moved outside of the cellular area and had no signal. I drove now like a mad woman closer to the building, nothing.

I jumped out of the car and attempted to push redial, I got them and again said, "I am so sorry!"

The call dropped again. We were given half an hour to do the interview and at this point I was down to five minutes. I ran into a little square foyer type area and dialed again.

They said "hello", I tried walking, but they told me they could not hear me, so I stood stark still in the corner of the little foyer.

I remember Simcha's British accent say, "Oh you sound like you are in a toilet", but they could hear me, and I could hear them and that is all that mattered.

Because we were short on time they said, "tell us why you want to come."

I did not dare tell them that I really didn't, and I was going to Scotland but since God had brought me this far, I prayed in my head for my answer.

Out came something like this:

"I want to come because I think I settle instead of expect God to show up. I think I am willing to take the leftovers instead of thinking God will show up extravagantly. I want the God of the extravagant and I know He wants to show me that is who He is. I want to break off my thinking that I am only worth settling for, I want the dump truck, not the little pieces. I want to know the God of extravagant."

They asked me if I would be okay with the following:

1) Climb a Mountain?

My answer was that I lived in the prairie, we do not even have any hills, so I would have to work on that one and I would join the gym – and I did.

2) Sleep in a Tent in the Desert?

I am a camper gal and that sounded like a lot of fun.

3) Swim in the Dead Sea?

Swimming is my favorite sport so no issues there.

They said, "we would like to extend an invitation for you to come."

I almost screamed out loud when they said that. I think it came out as, "Really? Really? You want me to come? This must be the worst interview of the whole pack and you still want me to come?"

They laughed and assured me that "yes" they wanted me to come.

Now, I was excited to go to Israel! I told them I was going to scream and do a dance and they asked if they could watch via the Whatsapp, to which I said a firm "no."

But I did run outside and scream and do a little dance and my excitement about going to Israel went from 0 to 60 in about five seconds! The trip was on and I was 100% invested.

One of the questions on the application form said, "can you afford this trip?" I guiltily lied and said yes, but only because God had told me I was going so I figured He had a plan. I did not have a clue about how.

I had mentioned to a group of ladies that I belong to that I had applied to go to Israel on this journey. I told no one about the money situation, the deposit or the fact I had no idea how I would get there.

The next meeting of the group of ladies there was an envelope on top of my Bible. I was about to open it when someone said, "NO! please do that later." Intrigued I wondered what was in it.

I opened the envelope later in the car and had to pull over to have a good cry because I was so overwhelmed. Inside the envelope was $600 cash for my trip to Israel. I had told no one except my hubby that in order to go on this trip, I was required to pay a $500 deposit in US funds immediately with the balance being due when I got to Israel in two months. God had blessed me with exactly the money I needed for the deposit to hold my spot.

I knew for sure that I was going to Israel!

God graciously gave me the remainder of the money through several different means, some friends, some tax return but He provided, and I had the money to go on my trip and even have some for spending while I was there. God of the extravagant had started to show up in providing His overwhelming provisions to His daughter.

Notes & Nuggets:

Notes & Nuggets:

CHAPTER 2

The Training

O ne of the requirements that was expected of us who were going to the program was to complete an online set of courses. It usually took about 200 hours, so they wanted you to start it as soon as possible in order to finish it before you got there.

I found the courses fascinating and I soaked up the information in the sessions like a sponge. The course covered many different topics, from the history of Israel to the Prophet Elijah and End Times Prophecy. We were asked not to share the info as they are working on completing the courses to be available to the public for a fee and have access to the same information. It will be worth it!

I will not tell you about the courses, rather I will tell you about the journey and things I discovered on the way and through the trip.

I was amazed at how over and over God chooses the underdog, the weak, the small to carry His message (like me).

He chose the Hebrew people, a small group of people, in a very small country to make big claims and statements about their God. Why could they make these statements? Because there was no way they could humanly do them, so it had to be God! The world has been against the Jewish nation since the beginning, putting them in bondage or slavery. It is not how we think a chosen people would be cared for, but it is somehow God's way.

Israel exists only because God said it does. Satan has been trying to destroy it since the beginning.

Only God could take 70 people into Egypt and bring 4-5 million people out despite persecution and in slavery.

He does things opposite to how we think they should be done. He reverses it.

"Now the Lord had said unto Abram, Get thee out of thy country, and from thy kindred, and from thy father's house, unto a land that I will shew thee: And I will make of thee a great nation, and I will bless thee, and make thy name great; and thou shalt be a blessing: And I will bless them that bless thee, and curse him that curseth thee: and in thee shall all families of the earth be blessed." Genesis 12:1–3

Gods desire, the Father's heart, is to Bless the World as He promised in the above Abrahamic Covenant. God said He could only do that through Abraham, the Jewish people. The world is so busy fighting the Jewish people that they have no idea; it is only through the Jewish people that the world will be blessed.

The disciples of Jesus were not chosen because they were great, they were great only because they were chosen. The same is true for you and me. The same is true for the Jewish nation. We do not get called because we can do great things for God, rather we become great when we realize we are children of God and in His strength, not ours, we can do great things.

The Kingdom of God is reversed to the kingdom of earth. In the world we live in, we ask for things because we need or want them; in God's Kingdom, we thank Him for the gifts He gives before we even receive them. Reverse order.

In the world, we try to earn our way, but God says we can Never earn our way, He prepares the way, we simply have to accept or reject it.

The disciples of Jesus day thought that Jesus would reign as an earthly King, when He was brutally killed, their dreams died. God brought Jesus back from the dead to restore the dreams, only God can do that. God reversed the order life after death.

In the church, we think we have to find ways to pull or attract people in, but I have discovered that God is pulling people out of the church. As radical as that may sound, as I watch around me it is true. The conventional church as we know it here in North American is stunted. It is not growing by leaps and bounds as it is in the Orient or along the Silk Road. The largest churches in the world are currently in Korea.

Yoido Full Gospel Church is a Pentecostal church in Seoul, South Korea, with about 800,000 members (2018).

In the music video *"Fire of Your Spirit"* by Sarah Liberman, the song that haunted my mind for a couple of months, Jesus comes to the woman in the video and touches her and leads her out of the tabernacle/church.

I think this is a hugely symbolic gesture, Jesus has anointed believers around the world to *"be the church"*. That means living out our life as a sacrifice to God, outside of the church building and being used by Him and for Him, everywhere we go. In a sense it means being a living example of "the church" to others around us.

People are not flocking to the church buildings anymore, rather they are encountering believers in their own settings, work, school, play. Believers need to be aware that they are being watched "as the church" to see how we fare in the world.

We are living in a time of unprecedented miracles and wonders; it is as if God is answering all kinds of prayers quicker and faster. God is answering the prayers that we have long ago given up on; that person, that situation that you knew would not change – they are changing!

God is wanting to blow our minds with Himself and He is doing it outside of the church building. He is showing up all over as the God of the Extravagant.

I keep hearing the phrase: God is wanting to bring heaven to earth.

The Lord's Prayer is coming true: "Your will be done on earth as it is in heaven..." Matthew 6:9-13

People keep wanting desperately to go to heaven, but God wants to bring heaven to earth, just like He did at the beginning of the Bible in Genesis. God walked with Adam and Eve in the garden of Eden.

Genesis 3:8 "And they heard the sound of the LORD God walking in the garden in the cool of the day, and the man and his wife hid themselves from the presence of the LORD God among the trees of the garden."

God's purpose never changed He wants heaven to be evident on earth, not in a church building, but in the "the people" He is building.

One of the awesome things in Israel was the unity of our group. We came together for two weeks, forty-two people from all over the world, different cultures, different churches, celebrating and worshipping the same God in unity.

We did not sit down and name our differences and prejudices, we were united as one man, one body this side of heaven. We took our eyes off each other and placed them solely on God. It was such a beautiful thing. We were all on level ground, equal.

We all started out by completing the training, in this way we all started out on level ground, on the same foundation that the leaders of our course wanted us to be on. God works powerfully when there is unity!

Often, we hear in sermons that everything is dependent on how we behave but God says everything is dependent on whose we are: His children, the children of God and how He sees us.

The world says love each other except of course your enemies and those who persecute you.

God says Love those who persecute you, especially your enemies.

"You have heard that it was said, 'Love your neighbor and hate your enemy.' But I tell you, love your enemies and pray for those who persecute you, that you may be children of your Father in heaven. He causes his sun to rise on the evil and the good and sends rain on the righteous and the unrighteous. If you love those who love you, what reward will you get? Are not even the tax collectors doing that? And if you greet only your own people, what are you doing more than others? Do not even pagans do that? Be perfect, therefore, as your heavenly Father is perfect." Matthew 5:43-48

This is the message of the nation Israel, living examples of God's grace. God has for thousands of years repeatedly rescued and redeemed the Jewish people. It is their pattern, their dance together.

In North America there has been taught in various churches something that is called a Replacement Theology. This teaching says that since the Jew's have rejected God, especially since they crucified Jesus, that the new church, the gentile Christians have taken precedence in the kingdom of God.

Actually, according to the Bible, the gentile (or non-Jewish) Christians have been grafted into the Jewish faith, and because of this they are able to receive the promises and blessings of God together with the

Jewish nation. Co-heirs, jointly sharing the same root system, not better, just different. (Romans 11:11-31)

When tree grafting is done in agriculture, a cutting of a one branch is taken, it is whittled down to allow a branch from another tree to join it and grow on it. You tape the two branches together and allow them to "heal together, to form a union". If you take an orange tree and graft an apple tree branch to it, each branch will still grow its own oranges and the other branch the apples. The grafting does not produce a "joint or hybrid" fruit. Each one still grows what it is supposed to, but they now share the roots. This is important to remember, we as gentile believers get to join the Jewish believers and share the common "root", namely Jesus, but we remain Jewish and Gentiles with the common name: believers in Jesus.

The Christian church is commanded to bless, and pray for Israel, the nation and the people, their co-heirs.

The world is in a time of intense pressure, it could be said we are in a "birthing time". A time where God wants to birth a new thing. Could it be that God wants to birth a new "church"?

Not a building, but a people. People who love under the hardest conditions, people who do not belong to one "building" rather they have church out in the world. A people who seem to grow with persecution and challenge. People who are different, with a faith that is unshakable with signs and wonders following them. A people who can say – the Kingdom of Heaven is being lived out down here earth.

When Jesus died, a little band of Jewish disciples, twelve in all, devoted their lives to spreading the message of Jesus. The result was the world, all around the world up to present day has been changed by the message spread by these handful of people. If God can change the world with a handful, think of what He can do with His much larger church today, we could be unstoppable!

Notes & Nuggets:

Notes & Nuggets:

CHAPTER 3

THE SOUND

The house I stayed in in Israel, was up on a hill and with a short walk we could walk to a look-out point staring out over the amazing Mediterranean Sea.

The house backed onto a zoo, yes, an actual animal zoo. One woman from another country once thought a woman was being murdered in the night because the peacocks yell out a "help" sound. The squawks, caw's, howling, growling and various other noises began as a constant annoyance and became something so much more. God used it as a valuable teaching lesson.

The very first night when our group got together in worship, God showed me something extraordinary. I believe totally and completely, that while I was physically sitting on a chair in the room, that my spirit was taken up to heaven. I have not had anything like this happen to me before so to try to describe it is hard. I now understand how hard it is was for Ezekiel, Paul, John and others in the Bible to try to describe something they had experienced or seen but they had nothing to compare it to.

As we, our group, were singing and worshipping God, I had my eyes closed and was focused on the voices in the room, joined together in worship. I cannot even recall what song we were singing or even an exact moment but suddenly I became aware that the voices had become increasingly louder and that so many more voices had seemed to join us. Our music, our sound, was reaching up to heaven and heaven was singing our song with us.

Did you get that? I had the privilege, the gift, of literally hearing heaven sing along with us. Please stay with me here and do not get caught up in the experience, and why her, or how does she know?

Please push that aside, because I have NO answers, the only thing I know is that I am to share what I experienced because God has a message for me and a message for you in it.

I have put off sharing this experience, I have been disobedient and selfish. God convicted me a week ago of being more afraid of man than Him. He let me know that I am being disobedient by not sharing the exceptional gift I was given and that He will replace me if I do not share what He has given me. I am compelled therefore to share this experience with you, you have to know.

I was shown: What we do here on earth, is known in heaven and that heaven is a very real place.

I was stunned that night when I realized something very weird was going on, I tried to look around me and realized that it was very dark and I could no longer see anyone or anything, but I could hear the singing, the magnificent singing! A true myriad of voices, not just those in the room. I realized at once, and again I am not sure how, that our singing had gone up to heaven and heaven had joined us and that I was no longer in that room. I felt no different, had no special sensations except the amazing gift of exceptional singing.

As I stood (I was standing in heaven although physically my body was sitting in the chair in the room) and absorbed the singing, I began to see above me in the dark expanse, red and white fireballs, looking much like fireworks or flashes of lightening. I thought at first that these fireworks were in celebration to our singing. I realized or it came to me, that our song had created in the heavens a bunch of red and white fireballs, I had no idea the significance.

I marveled at how wonderful and beautiful the fireworks were and then I noticed that the fireballs were being launched from pipes, similar looking to the ones in an old-fashioned music organ. I sensed and am not sure how, but I knew that these fireballs were not random, and they were not fireworks. They were intentional and targeted; they were very strategic, being launched, like strategic lightening balls. I stood there awestruck and mesmerized watching this spectacular display.

It seemed to me to be a long time that I was in this place watching the fireballs but when the song started to wind down, I found myself back in the original room, seated on my chair listening to the voices in the lit room singing praise to God. I looked around me to see if anyone had noticed that I had been missing or if they had noticed anything at all, perhaps to confirm that I was not crazy, but no one seemed to notice that anything was amiss.

I was so overcome by what had happened that the tears began to flow, in joy, gratitude, confusion and emotions. The leaders of the group kept looking at me with questioning looks as if to ask if I was okay. I cannot imagine what they were thinking about this woman from Canada: first night and she is already an emotional mess. I shared this experience with them a few days later but it would be five days later before I addressed our group about it.

The explanation from God about the vision did not come right away, the vision with the experience came and then that night God woke me up at 3:00 am to talk about it and "sound" became a theme for God and I throughout my trip to Israel.

In the 3:00 am download, I realized that our music was creating a weapon in the heavenlies. Those fireballs were weapons being shot at the enemy. The sounds we were making were being directly targeted at the enemy, satan and his kingdom.

I had never heard anything like this before, my brain threatened to explode from the gravity of the information and the upmost importance it was for people to know this.

As I lay there at 3:00am I heard the rooster start his daily cry down in the zoo. I heard in my spirit, the following question:

Q: How many people do you think can hear that one rooster?

A: I pondered this for a bit, we were in a residential area, so I guessed, hundreds or thousands. That rooster could be heard by thousands of people.

The next question that came was similar:

Q: How many people can hear the peacock cry out?

A: Again, I answered probably thousands.

Q: The last question was: How many people hear when we (believers) all sing together?

A: I honestly did not have a clue.

A: The answer came as: *millions*

People united in worship, singing praises to God, our music is heard on earth and in the heavens by millions. I was shocked.

God let me know that: *words are communication, but sound is connection.*

Words are equally important and have their own place in the universe. God's Word - the Bible, is communication, they are God's words to us, one of the ways He speaks to us.

Music – especially music in a united group of various believers is connection. It is this praise, this music, this sound, that connects heaven to earth. *It is sound that brings heaven to earth*.

God wants us to know that while many of us are longing and waiting to go to heaven, God wants to bring heaven down to earth!

Sound does that. Sound in heaven is used and not wasted. It is a commodity and it is a commandment:

"Shout for joy to the Lord, all the earth. Worship the Lord with gladness; come before Him with joyful songs" Psalm 100:1

"Enter his gates with thanksgiving and his courts with praise; give thanks to him and praise his name." Psalm 100:4

"And the ransomed of the Lord will return. They will enter Zion with singing; everlasting joy will crown their heads. Gladness and joy will overtake them, and sorrow and sighing will flee away." Isaiah 35:10

"Give thanks to the Lord, call on His name; make known among the nations what He has done, and proclaim that His name is exalted. Sing to the Lord, for He has done glorious things; let this be known to all the world. Shout aloud and sing for joy, people of Zion, for great is the Holy One of Israel among you." Isaiah 12: 4-6

When we sing to our King, the angels join us, and the sound vibrates the whole earth and the heavens. It is a mighty weapon in warfare that has huge, tearing down effects for strongholds and demonic defenses. **It is probably the most unused and misunderstood weapon available to us.**

In the Old Testament the armies of God marched out to battle with the worshippers, the trumpets, the music at the front of the line. It was a form of warfare.

Consider this quote:
"Based on a great number of studies, researchers claim that we all respond to music on a neurological level. Music affects our behavior, psychology and reality perception.
Music is used as a medical treatment to help those, who suffer from the effects of a stroke or other condition to recover.
Music affects the production of immunoglobulin A, an antibody that positively affects immunity, says other research, so why many music therapists claim that music is sometimes even more useful than pills.
It is less expensive and has no side effects, right? There are thousands of music therapists in the USA, who help people with mental problems or emotional trauma to overcome their problems, using music." https://www.renderforest.com/blog/does-music-affect-our-behavior, Renderforest Oct 1, 2018

Music heals, music is a weapon, music invades our souls, music is so much more than notes on a page! Music is one of the major keys to God's kingdom.

Music can go where preaching cannot, we can share the gospel without preaching simply by singing. Music is a universal language; it is everywhere on the planet. The words of a song carefully planted, can produce an abundant amount of harvest. We have this weapon that we do not use fully down here on earth.

But there is more...
When I was in Israel many of the messages I heard were about music and sound. God is waiting for us to use our sound.

God is calling up His church today, this very day, to rise up and start sharing our song/sound, to use our praise, to plant seeds, to breakdown strongholds and to help set people free. The world is waiting for us to walk in the power and anointing of God, sound is one of the anointings.

Power in the spiritual realm is dependent upon your prayer and praises. These two things create amazing power.

It's funny as we get older, we seem to lose interest in "sound", the music becomes too loud, too annoying, and yet music holds the power to change the atmosphere of both heaven and earth, we should never tire of it.

Heaven is waiting for your sound to join the chorus. You can make a difference with your voice.

In the book of Daniel, in the Old Testament, it says Daniel got down onto the floor to pray three times per day.

"Now when Daniel learned that the decree had been published, he went home to his upstairs room where the windows opened toward Jerusalem. Three times a day he got down on his knees and prayed, giving thanks to his God, just as he had done before." Daniel:6:10

Daniel, who even when it was forbidden by law, continued to honor God in prayer (sound), three times a day. I marvel that in North America a couple years ago there was a huge surge in following Daniel, it was based on the Biblical book of Daniel, called the Daniel diet or the Daniel fast, mimicking Daniel's eating patterns.

Where, I wonder, is the pattern mimicking Daniels praying patterns? Three times a day he got down on his knees and prayed. A very solemn question for us to consider and think about especially in light of this news that sound is connection with heaven and heaven is waiting to hear it.

When I was in Brussels waiting for my flight to Israel, I saw many Orthodox Jews go off by themselves to a corner and start praying in the airport because it was their custom to honor God many times a day. Why don't we?

The morning after my 3:00 am talk with God and the heavenly vision of the night before, I talked to my roommate about sound and music and she incredulously told me that she had heard the story of the same vision from two other people over in Israel in that past week.

This really got my attention, if God is doing a repeat of something it is truly something that He wants us to get! It is a message for the whole world.

On another day, I was standing out on the deck of the guest house listening to the worship music inside the room behind me. I could also hear the sounds of the zoo below me; a chorus of voices mixed with both animal and people sounds. I sensed that all these noises blend together and go up to heaven and that heaven is indeed a very noisy place, it has constant cries and sounds going up continuously to God.

At that moment in time, from where I was standing, heaven consisted of: the loud squawkers of the zoo, the many children yelling and crying, parents yelling, the praise music behind me, cries of people to other gods, the constant barrage of voices, the prayers, the pleas for help and guttural groanings. People and animal sounds blending together in a barrage of noise, travelling up to the heavenlies, and God hears and cares for the sounds and needs of each animal and person. That part in itself is mind blowing, that God hears and cares for all of us.

Then there are the sounds that cause heaven to stir! God is continuously listening, searching for the right "cry", the right "sound" that causes Him to turn His head, tilt it and listen. When He hears that sound, a smile spreads over His face, the sound delights Him; He then focuses His attention on it. God showed me that the heavens wait and listen for God's people to cry out and/or sing out to Him and to create their own powerful "sound": like we did that first night in the room, singing out and praising God.

35

I want to be intensely clear on this part: apart from the singing together in worship sound, there is another sound, a particular sound or tone that God went on to show me that was different than when we "sang together" and this was a very deliberate sound. I have hesitated to even write about this sound because I was not sure how to even describe it.

I wondered over in Israel and upon my return as to why I, me, was given this info about sound, why was I chosen to get a vision? I realized it was to share it, via my gifting, my writing. Remember: words are communication.

Words are communication – sound is connection.

I was so humbled that God chose to share this message with me that I looked for "sound" all over Israel.

Our touring group made this particular "sound or tone" four times over the ten days I was in Israel and it really is a "pitch" more so than a sound. When I say sound, people tend to think "volume", but this sound was more a tone or pitch. Not high or low, but a definite "note".

Remember this is different than unity of voices in song and praise. The very first night when I heard heaven sing with our group, I also heard this sound, in addition to the music we were singing. I did not know what it was at the time, I put it down to our "singing" but it was more than that.

The sound or pitch we made was not in a particular song, but rather it was made when the song lyrics ceased and we continued on each in our own voice, in our own way, singing out in unity to God. Our voices melted together into a certain "tone/pitch". It was an amazing sound. I only understood what this was after I had heard it a couple times.

The sound was attention grabbing, piercing to your soul much like the sound of roaring lion, a rooster crowing, a peacock crying out, a shofar blowing or a baby crying. You could call all these sounds loud, but it was not the loudness. You could call all these sounds "sharp", but it was not the sharpness. All of these sounds get your attention immediately, they call your spirit to attention. They are distinct and you know what they are the instant you hear them. This God sound does the same thing.

I definitely heard this same "sound" when our group went into the city of Jerusalem. I was sitting in the Garden of Gethsemane having a delightful quiet time, just me and God. All of the sudden a booming sound came out of a loudspeaker over at the Temple Mount calling all the Muslims to prayer. That sound disrupts the airwaves, the thought processes, and makes it hard to think, concentrate or pray until that sound stops. This was my first encounter with the Muslims' call to prayer.

It is called The Adhan. An Arabic word that means "to listen."

God and the angels wait and listen for their "sound" and come to attention when they hear it; satan and his army also wait for "their" sound and revel in it when his followers call out to him, taking over the airwaves of the physical territory.

The blaring loudspeaker I heard in the Garden of Gethsemane, calling Muslims to pray, the Adhan, was that sound, that exact pitch. The exact pitch that calls out to the enemy's camp five times a day, seven days a week.

Satan in his own realm stands and waits and when he hears that sound, he too cocks his head and hears the sound of his people calling out to him (unbeknown to the people, for they have been deceived thinking they are reaching Allah. The one and only God of the Islam faith). Satan and his army listen for their voices and join in with them, invest with them, encourage them and strengthen them.

There is no formal call to prayer for Believers of Jesus, whether you are Messianic Jew or a Jesus following Gentile. Unlike the Muslim's, God's people usually only call out a couple times a week at best, and often only one day a week – albeit Saturday or Sunday whichever day your congregation celebrates on and the rest of the week is fairly quiet. But God and the angels are waiting.

The whole middle east, all the countries surrounding Israel, call out five times a day giving air supremacy and territory to satan and his followers. If you have read the Bible – you know there are only two camps. You are either in Gods (Yahweh) camp or in the other camp and it is very clear about who runs the other camp. Please do not hate the messenger, I am simply conveying what it says in the Bible and the message given to me.

God is calling all Believers, Christians and Messianic Jews worldwide to listen, to step up and call out to Him in music and communal worship times more than once a day and most definitely more than once a week. Perhaps we too can take up the Daniel Challenge and call out to God on our knees three times a day filling the atmosphere with God's sound.

I have continued to look for sound upon my return from Israel. I have heard a few sermons and several musicians talk about sound and they have the same message I received about the powerful sound of music and song. When God wants His message shared, He does not use one person, He used many! This is one of the many ways I knew the message I received was confirmed and that God wanted me to share my experiences.

The number one song on the Christian billboard charts right now (August/September 2019) and has been for a few weeks is *"Raise a Hallelujah"* by Jonathan and Mellisa Helser.

In the middle of that song, Jonathan says, "Just begin to raise your own Hallelujah, I can't do it for you. There's a song written on your heart that only you can sing. And when you sing enemies flee, when you sing prison walls come falling down, when you sing, heaven invades the earth".

I could not have said it any better myself because truly, that my friends ***is the "sound" of heaven*** joining earth and the effects of our sound in the heavenly places.

The song, *"Raise A Hallelujah"* itself is so powerful – please read or listen to the story behind the song and you will know that sound can produce miracles. Two children are alive today because that song was sung over them and heaven heard, and miracles were produced. Sound is a powerful weapon![1]

But this is not news to God – read what happened to the walls of Jericho back in the Old Testament. Joshua 6: 1-20

"Now the gates of Jericho were securely barred because of the Israelites. No one went out and no one came in.
[2] Then the Lord said to Joshua, "See, I have delivered Jericho into your hands, along with its king and its fighting men. [3] March around the city once with all the armed men. Do this for six days. [4] Have seven priests carry trumpets of rams' horns in front of the ark. On the seventh day, march around the city seven times, with the priests blowing the trumpets. [5] When you hear them sound a long blast on the trumpets, have the whole army give a loud shout; then the wall of the city will collapse and the army will go up, everyone straight in."
[6] So Joshua son of Nun called the priests and said to them, "Take up the ark of the covenant of the Lord and have seven priests carry trumpets in front of it." [7] And he ordered the army, "Advance! March around the city, with an armed guard going ahead of the ark of the Lord."
[8] When Joshua had spoken to the people, the seven priests carrying the seven trumpets before the Lord went forward, blowing their

---

[1]   https://godtv.com/the-powerful-testimony-behind-bethel-musics-new-song-raise-a-hallelujah/

trumpets, and the ark of the Lord's covenant followed them. 9 The armed guard marched ahead of the priests who blew the trumpets, and the rear guard followed the ark. All this time the trumpets were sounding. 10 But Joshua had commanded the army, "Do not give a war cry, do not raise your voices, do not say a word until the day I tell you to shout. Then shout!" 11 So he had the ark of the Lord carried around the city, circling it once. Then the army returned to camp and spent the night there.

12 Joshua got up early the next morning and the priests took up the ark of the Lord. 13 The seven priests carrying the seven trumpets went forward, marching before the ark of the Lord and blowing the trumpets. The armed men went ahead of them and the rear guard followed the ark of the Lord, while the trumpets kept sounding. 14 So on the second day they marched around the city once and returned to the camp. They did this for six days.

15 On the seventh day, they got up at daybreak and marched around the city seven times in the same manner, except that on that day they circled the city seven times. 16 The seventh time around, when the priests sounded the trumpet blast, Joshua commanded the army, "Shout! For the Lord has given you the city! 17 The city and all that is in it are to be devoted to the Lord...

20 When the trumpets sounded, the army shouted, and at the sound of the trumpet, when the men gave a loud shout, the wall collapsed; so everyone charged straight in, and they took the city."

The message about sound is not new, nor is it a message for "me", it is for all of us. God is reminding us in Joshua 6 of what He has already given us. The significance of sound as a weapon seems to have lost significance down through the ages. Sound matters.

The Messianic church I was privileged to be a part of for those 10 days in Israel with amazing worship leaders – they already knew the power of sound. God is using them mightily around the world, while they had not heard about the fireballs, they knew the power of sound, song and praise.

One of the reasons Israel is such a divided nation is because of sound. If God's people united together in times of worship and times of communal "sound", the power of God would push back the powers of darkness over the middle east and from wherever the believers were worshiping. Enemies walls would fall down, enemies will flee, and the power of God will invade the land. It only takes a remnant, a few who will faithfully release God's sound over the land.

When God's children call out with the sound of praise, united in a chorus of sound, all of heaven comes to attention and they turn, and they join in. They are drawn to the sound and they join with us, fight with us, encourage us and strengthen us.

Sound is infectious, it invades your soul and the souls of others.

God works multi-dimensionally, what I mean by this is that He is not limited to one dimension. It would stand to reason that if music and sound can tear down physical walls like Jericho, and it can tear down and destroy strongholds of the enemy, then it should also be true that music can work inside of us, physically, as well.

42

To survive in life often we can become hardened in our hearts, we build walls to protect our self from others and the hurts that life can throw at us. God can use music to help tear down those walls that you have helped build around your heart. God has given us the key to opening the door to our hearts and setting ourselves free!

By using praise and worshipping God, we allow God access to our hearts spiritually, reaching areas that we perhaps did not even know were closed off. Let God have access to your hearts, as you are singing and praising Him, tell Him you want those walls torn down, those hardened areas washed clean. Start using music as a weapon.

Sound is connection between heaven and earth. Sound is connection between you and God.

Unity in adoration and praise is a powerful tool to infect yourself and others – believers or not. Your sound can change the atmosphere, the climate in any situations. While in Israel, I heard stories of how believers took their music into the other nations surrounding Israel, nations that would be described as hostile to Jews and Believers. When the musicians sang, whoever was in hearing started singing out with them in praise, it was infectious, even if they did not know what the words meant.

I struggled a lot with this whole concept of sound while in Israel, I was not sure what to do with it and it seemed so important and so huge. It became clearer when a dear friend of mine in Israel, Lisa said, "God uses our differences and uniqueness' much like an orchestra, made up of many instruments, to create a beautiful and perfect song/sound." Yes! That is very much how sounds works. We each have a very important part to sing.

In the words of Ephesians 5:18-20

> *"Instead, be filled with the Spirit, speaking to one another with psalms, hymns, and songs from the Spirit. Sing and make music from your heart to the Lord, always giving thanks to God the Father for everything, in the name of our Lord Jesus Christ."*

If your praise and worship of God is a weapon, now that you know, will you use it?

Not just on Sunday, will you use your voice every day? Will you call out in prayer like Daniel three times a day? Will you raise your voice and be part of the sound that heaven needs to hear?

Crank up the praise music and let 'er rip, because heaven is waiting to connect!

Notes & Nuggets:

Notes & Nuggets:

CHAPTER 4

THE LAND

I srael is a land of contrasts: the ancient to the new, the many different cultures, the modern to the nomadic (Bedouin's), the peaceful versus the threat of war at every turn and then there are all the religions.....

I jotted down my first impressions of Israel: old, green, the lush tropical foliage. There was the dirty, old sections and the new, modern buildings, such a wide contrast, but everything was orderly, friendly, and proud.

There is tension inside of Israel, but I would say that the big tension everyone talks about is coming from the outside of the country of

47

Israel and it is very real. The Israeli's are expecting a war at any moment and they have lived this way for centuries.

It was stated to me that other world powers are the ones deciding the fate of Israel, not Israel itself.

Israel is a hospitable nation and very safe for a woman travelling alone. I never felt uncomfortable or unsafe. When I landed in Israel and got to the train platform by the airport and found all the writing in Hebrew I was taken aback as to how to find where I was going if I did not speak the language. There was a young man there who helped me and sent me in the right direction. (I learned after that if you wait long enough the writing will also appear in English).

When I got to the platform it was "rush hour" 4:00 pm and lots of people. I asked one lady if she spoke English and most do, she said to stay by her, and she would help me get to the right station. She informed me how to make sure you got in the flow to get on. This is the "crush": one door and people getting on and off at the same time with only minutes until the train pulls away.

My new friend was getting off the train before my stop and instructed another Jewish woman to inform me when to get off the train. This new lady took up the task and told me when I was two stops away, this conversation sparked interest in our little cabin on the train. By the time I was ready to get off, a soldier had pulled down my luggage from the rack, three people had been asked to move and I was set in place by the door to ensure my departure. I marveled at how hospitable they had been.

Travelling home to Canada with a friend, we were sitting at the train platform waiting for the train when we heard the announcement that the train would arrive at platform 2. I started to look around and platform 2 was on the other side of the tracks with a huge wire fence in between us and it. I told my friend I think we are at the wrong place. Three soldiers had come around the corner and we asked where platform 2 was. They said we had to run to the stairs and go underneath to the other side. We started running but heard the train come and go before we got to the other side. We were discouraged and not sure what to do to reach the airport in time. The three soldiers stayed right with us and all whipped out their phones had a conversation and then replied, "we will stay with you, you come with us and we will take you to the airport. If we take the next train, we will stay with you until the transfer to the new train to the airport."

Wow, *"we will stay with you"* – can you believe that? These kids were willing to babysit a couple middle aged foreign ladies. We ended up figuring out when another train that would go direct to the airport would come and realized that we would only be ten minutes behind schedule so we said we would take that one and graciously declined their amazing offer to stay with us.

The number of military personnel took me by surprise. Kids walking around casually with huge machine guns strapped around their necks; it used to be video games. In Israel it is mandatory for all young people aged 18-21 to go into the army, regardless of religion or beliefs, they join together as comrades. Boys sign up for three years and girls for two. My taxi driver, an Arab told me about his kids in the army, his young son had just gone into the army and he was missing him, but it is the duty of all Israeli's to send your children and they are very proud to do that. He himself had been in the army and had to keep going back once a year for a short time until he was released at the age of 40.

Is there tension in the land? Oh yes, I heard the Israeli military flying overhead every day and on days where you heard it more than four times (up to ten) you knew something was going on somewhere. Many places had reminder posters up to pray for the army, their children.

We often hear about the Gaza strip here in North America. It was explained to me that the fight over this little strip of land is because of the terrorist group, Hamas. It is the gateway from Egypt to Israel and the middle east and is the highway for terrorist activity. The civilians living in Gaza, 1.5 million would love to get out but Hamas needs to the civilians as protection. If there were no civilians living there, Israel would simply wipe out Hamas. The civilians get used by Hamas as pawns who push them, especially children and teens up front and then when civilians die in the conflict, the world blames Israel. There is a saying I heard: When Hamas starts loving their people more than hating the Jews the fighting will stop.

This tiny little county of Israel is surrounded by enemies, from my travels there I literally could see Lebanon, Syria, Jordan. On the other side of the borders, are hostile enemy countries waiting and wanting to try to come in.

Jerusalem is another matter; the fight for the land of the dome of the rock and this city is very real and has been contested for centuries by many governments and religions, this fight will not go away quietly or without some conflict. This is probably the most sought-after piece of real estate in the world.

Everything in Israel is "up", the topography of Israel, hills, mountains makes all things be "up". You go up to Jerusalem.   I imagine that in Biblical times, those calf muscles would be in great shape because you walked everywhere unless you had a donkey or camel (and I saw both).

I spent a lot of my travel time watching from the bus window for sheep and shepherds. I wanted to take a picture of a "real" shepherd. Animals dotted the land on the hillside, often I would see the sheep and goats but no shepherds were in view. My travel companion asked me what I was watching for and I said, "I am watching for my shepherd."

She replied, "me too." She grinned with the implication that she was watching for the return of her shepherd, Jesus.

Jerusalem is a huge bustling city; I loved the markets – rows and rows of stalls selling everything from food and spices to handbags and shoes. You could spend days at the market and not see everything. Boisterous stall peddlers calling out to come and see in their shop, offering the best deals, "but only for you", truly fun. If you are a people watcher Jerusalem is the place for you to sit back and enjoy.

I was shocked and not prepared at the graveyard in Jerusalem. A massive hillside that stretches out across from the Temple Mount and across from the Garden of Gethsemane, bordering the city, with all these cement-like boxes, tombs, scattered all over it. Thousands and thousands and thousands of boxes.

Canada being a relatively new country and not so many people to bury has soft ground where we can dig and bury our caskets underground. I was not used to seeing boxes on top of the hard ground that is too hard to dig in and 3,000+ years' worth of tombs.

Sitting alone in my thoughts in the exquisite beauty of the Garden of Gethsemane, looking out over the massive graveyard, hearing the loudspeakers calling Muslims to prayer, I truly marveled at the mighty contrasts of this little land.

Much like the land, the people of Israel are diverse. I was introduced to Orthodox Jews, Messianic Jews, Arabs-Muslims, Bhai, Druze, Bedouins, and Russians, each group has such an intricate history surrounding their culture and beliefs and all living peacefully in the country of Israel.

One of the most curious things for me in Israel was seeing the huge apartment buildings, either standing empty or being built, with towering cranes scattered all around the cities. I questioned what all these empty buildings were for.

I was told that these buildings are for the returning Jewish people when they come home from all over the world, the term used is: **making Aliyah** (moving to the land of Israel)

Israel's population stands at 8,972,000 at the end of 2018, 174,000 more people than a year before, the Central Bureau of Statistics said, of that number, 6,668,000 (74.3%) are Jews, 1,878,000 are Arabs (20.9%) and 426,000 (4.8%) are other.

Out of the 14.5 million Jewish people in the world, 46% reside in Israel. The Jewish population of Israel now exceeds that of the <ins>United States</ins> by roughly one million.

(info from: https://www.jewishvirtuallibrary.org/latest-population-statistics-for-israel)

The Law of Return – making Aliyah. The Law of Return is a rule enacted by the Israeli government in 1950 that allows all Jews, both ethnic and religious, to return to Israel as their homeland and gain citizenship.

- This law was created largely to create a route to safety for Jews who were misplaced by the Holocaust, and for their descendants.

- A returning Jew is called an *oleh* (male) or *olah* (female).

The Jewish Agency for Israel in 2018 alone helped more than 30,000 Jews start new lives in Israel after making Aliyah. There are free one-way flights offered to Jewish people and their family for their flights home.

The Jewish Agency for Israel helps bring them home. All Jews, no matter where they were born, are Israeli citizens by right.

I was astounded at how many buildings were built and simply waiting for people to come and but saddened to learn that if you were a Messianic Jew, a Jew who believes that Jesus was the Messiah, you were refused entrance into the country even if you could prove that you had Jewish lineage.

The government building that made the decisions on who to let in and who not was in the city of Haifa. As a group we went and prayed over this building that they would start to let in Messianic Jews into the country for the Law of Return.

Israel is a very small country. Israel stretches 424 km (263 mi) from north to south, and its width ranges from 114 km (71 mi) to, at its narrowest point, 15 km (9.3 mi) and yet it is a land of deserts, lushness, farming, fishing, hills and mountains. Israel has a bit of everything in terms of topography and because it is so small you may have desert and farmland within a few miles of each other. There is the dead sea being lower than sea level and the wonderful coastline of the Mediterranean Sea and then on up to Mount Meron being the highest point at 1,208 meters (3,963 feet).

Sarah, one of our leaders, said to us that you cannot conquer new ground unless you hold the ground that God already gave you. This is a great challenge in Israel and also for us personally: Are you holding the ground God has given to you already? Stand firm on that ground and then reach for the new.

What ground has He given you? What land, physical property has He blessed you with? What about spiritual land, gifts, talents? Do you have family descendant land passed down from generation to generation? In Biblical times, the family passed the land, and their blessings down to their sons.

What town has God placed you in? Do you pray for the town government? Do you pray for your neighbors? Do you pray for your province or state? Do you pray for your country and lift the government to God on a regular basis – even if you do not like them? This is what holding the ground means and looks like.

What money, financial ground, has God given you? Are you a wise steward of it or do you hoard it for yourself? Are you satisfied or driven to make more? This is what holding the ground looks like for money.

What about familiar ground, for example: your family? Are you holding the ground with your descendants? Even if your children are not walking with God, are you on your knees upholding them before God every day, claiming God's promises over them. This is what holding the ground looks like.

We were challenged to consider what else is sharing the space with God. If we are not praying for all of the above, then we are not holding the land and something else is sharing it. Quite a sobering thought if we truly considered this question.

Hold the ground God has already given you. The Jewish people are trying to hold the ground God has given them.

Spiritually if you are not holding the ground around you and where you live, someone else is.

Consider this: there is not patch of land or ground that is not claimed spiritually. God is multi-dimensional, please remember that He works on different levels at the same time. Since there are only two kingdoms, Gods and satans, that ground or territory belongs to one of those two camps. Which camp do you live in? Are you fighting spiritually in prayer for this territory, this land that surrounds you?

The other ground to consider is the ground of your mind and your heart. This ground is most important because if our hearts and minds belong to God, if God is at its center, the physical ground or territory can be taken much easier. This is your place in God's kingdom, do not let satan steal it!

The ground of our mind and heart, is the ground that would best be described as a battleground. Thoughts, ideas, dreams, emotions, learning, people, jobs, children, spouses, family, all of these things battle for a place in your life. Is it wrong to have these things in our life? No, but it is wrong if any of these things takes the control of your mind or heart before God.

If you are not sure about this: Take one or two days and write down how much time you spend doing certain things. Bible reading, praying, eating, working, sleeping, bathroom, tv, reading, computer, phone, online games or groups, exercising. After you have done this, divide the day into waking hours. Say you have 12 hours of wake time. In that 12 hours, what took the most of your time? Number them 1 and down in order of highest time to lowest.   I bet, and I pray I am wrong, that our time with God and Bible reading and prayer, was the lowest number in our day and then we wonder why we have no spiritual power and other things have taken over our spiritual and physical ground. You have to be plugged into the power source to get the power.

If I give more space to Facebook than the Godbook (Bible) guess what has more influence in my day?   We say I do not have enough time in my day, it may be a matter of what I chose to spend my time on.

Your destiny and that of your family, is at stake by every decision you make; that is a daunting idea. God is multigenerational. It is not just about you! You whole family line and future generations are at stake by what ground you chose to keep and take.

I struggled with this over in Israel. I felt that it was just about me and I had given up on hopes and dreams for a bigger picture. I had put my hopes and dreams into a box and buried them just like the huge graveyard surrounding Jerusalem. Dead and gone. Jesus was there encouraging me to dig my hopes and dreams up and resurrect them. I felt like He was telling me to take back the land of my dreams. I was deeply afraid to, because I had had my hopes dashed before.

God assured me that it is not wrong to have dreams. God said He does not want to kill "Jane", He does not want Jane dead (and I have had teaching to this effect, die to self, where I cease to exist). God said He wants to *free Jane to use at His leisure, not His command*. He cares for Janes' heart and the desires that He put in there are from Him, therefore they are not wrong and are totally okay to have.

Yes, He wants to use me, but He also has plans to bless me and the two can co-exist in the land of the living.

Jewish people have all been in the army, they have been trained since teenagers to be warriors. They have had to learn by living under hostile rulers, take overs, and persecution, how to be fighters, how to live with hope, even when you cannot see any. The Jewish people are survivors, a strong, proud people who rise to the challenge.

This requires a warrior mentality, a mentality that says "not today satan" as he tries to move you to a passive, discouraged, slave mentality. The Israelites were forcibly persuaded to adopt a slave mentality when they were slaves in Egypt, then again under the Babylonians, also the Romans of Jesus time, and the Germans of WW 2, the list of persecutors is long. Some gave up and gave in, others never gave up hope, never gave up on God in spite of what their eyes saw before them. These are the ones who survived and kept the remnant of Israel alive.

What does it take to have a warrior spirit? Everything that God does is upside down to the world around us. A warrior in our world today fights, physically.

A warrior in God's kingdom, surrenders. We surrender on our knees or on our faces to God's plan, God's promises, we do not let anyone steal our relationship with Him, we do not let anyone steal our identity as God's child.

The very same Holy Spirit that raised Jesus from the dead is alive and working in the lives of His people. He does not come and go; He is there available inside of us 24 hours per day. With the Holy Spirit we are on the same level ground as Paul, Peter, Stephen, James,

Abraham, Moses, Elijah, for it was not the men who were special, but the God who called them.

This is the God who took a handful of people into Egypt and brought millions out, in spite of persecution. This is the God we serve.

What is dead in your land? What dreams, hopes, relationships have you given up on?

Whatever it is, God is saying, do not give up; take the land, pray into your dreams, declare God's promises, standing firm because of places like Israel.

A country and people that have survived the brutality of other nations, the tearing apart of the country but they prevail, they hold on. Why? Because God said *"go take the land"* Deuteronomy 1:8 and they are trusting Him.

Notes & Nuggets:

Notes & Nuggets:

CHAPTER 5

THE DESERT

I was not aware that there are four words in Hebrew that mean desert, English only has one so in translations in the Bible the true meaning of the word *desert* can get quite lost.

Our tour guide explained to us that the word "desert" can mean:
1) to speak: be ready to hear
2) leader/leadership: the one who speaks is the leader
3) to eliminate everything in the way: exterminator, to clear the ground
4) suitable place for flocks: the pasture for flocks

It was pointed out on my trip, that the desert is actually a place to prepare us for the Lord, an opportunity, not a punishment.

Moses was sent to the desert for 40 years to prepare him to go back to Egypt to save his people. He worked as a shepherd for his father-in-law Jethro.

The Israelites wandered in the desert for 40 years before they got to the promised land, having spent years in preparation.

Jesus went into the "wilderness" which was more than likely the desert and was tempted for 40 days by satan before He started His ministry.

John the Baptist who came from the wilderness, more than likely the desert, and spent 30 years being prepared by the Lord for ministry. Did John ever leave the desert? It is possible that he did not, as his ministry took place in the desert, he did not go seeking crowds, people came to him. John the Baptist sought only God and God sent the people to him. John's whole ministry was preparing people for God.

The desert is a place of preparation. The desert is not a place to try get out of, it is a place of growth, cultivation and purpose, it is a place to remain hidden, to grow more intimate with God. In the desert, there are fewer distractions, so it is not so difficult to concentrate on God.

Personally, I was not aware that desert and dry place were two entirely different places. The desert still gets some rain, approximately 20 mm per year, so it does have life in it.

The dry place has no rain which means no life, barren.

My first five days in Israel were in the beginning of April, we were met with a lot of rain and I hated it because I was so cold, I even had to go and buy warmer clothes. The country around me was rejoicing because rain is seen as a blessing in the land. In fact, the country of Israel had had five-six years of draught and they had been praying for rain. They were loving the rain! (it was a total perspective thing and I too eventually came to see the rain as a blessing).

Our group travelled into the desert and for two nights and we camped at a Bedouin campground, complete with Bedouin tents and food.

Upon entering my little tent, I noticed that on my pillow was a piece of dried poop from some kind of animal, this made me a little skeptical of the desert experience! But being a camper for years, I picked up the pillow took it to the tent entrance and flicked off the poop, then returned the pillow and simply turned it over. I then, searched the entire tent for any signs, traces of an animal, not finding anything else, I zipped up the tent and went on my way. A true desert adventure!

The food on my trip was absolutely a delight wherever we went, and the desert was no exception. The dishes were made with either goat or sheep cheese, the latter I found to be very strong tasting. I was a little taken back when we were brought a wonderful exquisite cup of tea and we spent quite a while trying to decipher what kind of amazing and exotic desert herbs or plants from the land the taste was. When I asked at the kitchen, she took out a box of store-bought tea called Lemon Lime... even the desert has some modern convenience.

We were driven to a place beside a Wadi (a dried stream/riverbed) to sit, be quiet and think. The desert is rocky, not sandy like I imagined and finding a comfy spot to sit without sharp rocks was the first order of business.

I sat for a while staring at the rocky cliffs all around me seeing only dirt and rocks. After a while I noticed the rocks at the top of the cliffs are small, pebble type rocks but as they came down the cliff the rocks they got bigger and at the bottom by the edge of the Wadi, they were large boulders, bigger than I could carry. The really big ones fell into the Wadi, the riverbed, and will get swept away when the Wadi floods.

You see, Wadi's kill a number of people every year in the middle east, even though they look harmless. Remember it was raining my first five days in Israel. A flash flood is a normal thing in the drylands. The arid ground is so dry and hard that the water does not seep in, it plunges down the Wadi's without any kind of notice, sweeping away everything in its path. Warnings about the danger of Wadi's are posted all around Israel.

The Wadi – a place where the nourishing and refreshing rain hits the hard ground, and instead of soaking in and saturating the ground with much needed moisture, the hard ground cannot accept it and it creates a wall of water, a flash flood, washing all moveable things in its path. Could this be the condition of many human hearts? God sends relief, He sends His peace, He sends His love, but our hearts are so hard that the nourishment, His peace, is not received, instead it runs off and washes away into barrenness.

Are we able to see it in ourselves, when our "ground" is hard? The places we need touching are the exact conditions of a desert, arid, dry and non-yielding.

I was sitting staring up at the rocky cliffs and I pondered: our problems and our trials, we all get them, they start as pebbles, as we dwell on them, stew and mull over them, they get larger. We try to fix them, make plans, all the while continuing to dwell on the problem, giving it life and space in our hearts and minds. Doing this, the problem can get even larger until it becomes boulders that weigh us down, we cannot carry that weight and they eventually cripple us or squeeze the life out of us.

The Bible says in 1 Peter 5:7a, *"cast your cares on Him"* – throw them into the Wadi!

Let God take over the problem and let Him take care of it and wash it away. Sound easy? Probably not as easy as we would like it to be, but it is true that whatever we dwell on will take over our life and turn into boulders that are too great for us to handle. These can be some of the items sharing "space" with God in our life.

---

*Jesus says He is "living water" in John 4:10 "If you knew the gift of God and who it is that asks you for a drink, you would have asked him and he would have given you **living water**"*

Jesus is the refreshing water of nourishment that the desert and you and I need. He is the water that can take rough ugly rocks and boulders and tumble them in the living water to produce a finished product of a beautifully polished and shiny gem. He is the one able to provide the water slowly, a bit at a time, enough to survive on or He can provide His living water in a fast and furious force (like a Wadi) that can drench you with soul nourishment in an instant. The condition of your heart will perhaps decide if your time will be long or short in the desert.

As I was sitting there in the desert staring at the rocks and cliffs, I noticed a little plant with yellow flowers down by my feet. There is life in the desert. I started to stare around at the ground, and I noticed more little plants, more little yellow flowers. These plants were not big, just small compact but I wondered, which plant was the first one that settled there, planting itself into the crags of the rocks.

It survived, grew, bore seeds and scattered its seeds all around the desert bringing patches of life to the landscape.

It astounded me when I started to look around, how much vegetation was all around me, sitting there in what I thought was a barren rocky desert.

We, you and I can be that one seed that settles in, grows where we are planted and spreads our seeds over a barren landscape all around us, to share and bring life to the environment.

On our way back to the bus, several of us noticed this unusual flock of rather large birds hovering above the hills of the Wadi. They appeared to be flying around in circles. At first notice we all thought they were vultures, circling around some kind of prey. Back on the bus, we were asked if we noticed the birds, apparently it was a very rare phenomenon and they were actually storks, millions of them on a migration path, we were very blessed to have seen them. God of the extravagant was showing up again.

Our tour guides told us that we were most privileged to see the phenomenon's of nature that we had: we had the rain that was breaking the years of draught and seeing the storks. They went on to tell us that a few weeks prior to our trip, 700 million butterflies did a one-day migration through Israel, these were all supernatural signs that pointed to God's blessing of Israel. They believed that God was pointing nature to Israel to capture people's attention to see what He is up to.

After the desert we went to the En Gedi Nature Reserve. Located on the eastern edge of the Judean desert, at the westside of the Dead Sea and overlooking it, is a most beautiful oasis, called En Gedi. En Gedi is a true oasis in the desert. The contrast is not lost on you. In the almost barren desert, overlooking the Dead Sea where nothing can live, is a garden of God, alive with life and promise.

En Gedi Nature Reserve is made up of two valleys, it boasts of four freshwater springs that have run for literally thousands of years, watering the landscape of the desert, creating a place of beauty, and sustaining life. Animals live alongside the springs as they provide water for the plants and shrubs to grow offering up water and food. There are old synagogue ruins on the property which you can go and view.

En Gedi is famous for its date palms and balsam trees. According to historical records, the balsam trees famous for their perfume, said to be the most expensive perfume plant ever. It was cultivated into groves at En Gedi and have been mentioned in Greek, Roman, and Egyptian writings from thousands of years ago. Mark Anthony was said to give a special gift of Balsam perfume to Cleopatra.

It became such a sought-after plant, but the Jewish people pulled up all the plants when their country was taken over by their enemies. The secret of how to cultivate, grow and get the perfume died out. In 1970 they were trying to re-establish the growth of Balsam trees, but it failed, and again in the 1990's and in 2003. God's gift to the Jewish people will stay buried.

Alongside Wadi David that we walked along, we saw Ibex, called wild goats but they looked to me, more like what we would call a small antelope. They were munching on the small shrubs that grow beside the spring.

I waded into the spring, it was not really deep, approximately knee height and probably 3-4 feet wide at its largest width. But once I put my foot in and felt the coldness of the water, I knew this was not "land" water, this water was coming from some place underground that kept it cold. What a gift, cold fresh water running through the hot and dry desert.

As we walked alongside the spring on a trail, I was astounded by the growth of the plant life. Appearing out of nowhere there are plants, reeds, palm trees, flowers and grass. We hiked up a trail that led up to a waterfall at the end of the canyon. The canyon has high sheer sided cliffs and are absolutely covered with rocks, crags and caves.

The Bible says King David hid out from Saul somewhere at En Gedi and you can see why (1 Samuel 23, 24). There are hiding places all over. Caves adorned the hillside and naturally made tunnels caused by reeds growing over and across the trail much like a child's "fort", hiding all who are beneath it. The canyon itself becomes a barrier to prevent a person from being able to cross from one side to the other, huge boulders to hide behind or beside dot the landscape. The realization that we were in an area that King David could have hid out in was exhilarating. Standing there looking around me seeing the hiding spots, I knew, it was just the place that could do it.

It was probably a place like or was En Gedi that Elijah was sent where the ravens fed and cared for him (1 Kings 17:2-16). You can picture the serenity Elijah would have felt, being fed by the birds and drinking from the cool water for refreshment, hiding from the oppressive heat in one of the caves.

The archeological findings from 4,000 BC around the En Gedi point to the fact that it has been giving life and sustenance to people and animals for a very long time.

It started to rain on us as we headed out of the canyon we had hiked into. Our leaders were shocked and told us that was a true miracle, because it rarely ever rains in the desert and we were being very blessed to be witnessing it. God of the extravagant had shown up again.

It was not lost on me that from my perspective, "rain" was not that much of a blessing. In Canada, rain is rain. Is Israel, "rain" is life. I wondered how many blessings I have missed over the years because my point of view or my perspective was not in the right place and I missed the miracles because of it.

We talk often in our Christian walk about going through "desert times" or "dry times" when we find a void of God in our lives. What if we instead looked at the desert as a place of solitude, a place of dry but not void of life, a place of hiding and growing.

It is a place of opportunity and it can be a refreshing place. The desert is not to be feared, it is an opportunity to rest, grow and be refreshed.

It is a place where we should leave the desert more filled with God than when we first went in, empowered and full.

Notes & Nuggets:

Notes & Nuggets:

CHAPTER 6

THE GARDEN & DISTRACTIONS

W e boarded a bus in Jerusalem to be taken to the outskirts, to the Mount of Olives and the Garden of Gethsemane, I did not know what to expect of this garden. I did not think that the original garden where Jesus walked could still be intact for over 2,000 years.

I looked back from the bus at the noisy, busy chaos that is Jerusalem and pondered why I could not seem to feel God's presence there. I could sense lots of spiritual activity but could not feel God's presence.

It occurred to me that Jerusalem is so noisy, and busy so I asked God where He was, because this was Israel after all, His chosen country,

His chosen people. We were passing a little hillside that was enclosed by a fence and I heard that inner voice say, " *I am here.*"

I had no idea where we were since I was a foreigner, but I felt a peace come over me as we drove by this grassy treed slope and I felt closer to God at that spot. I was sure we had arrived at the Garden of Gethsemane, but we had not.

We arrived at the Garden of Gethsemane and we had to walk in on a trail to enter the garden. The garden is now taken care of by another religious organization and it is stunningly beautiful. There are huge towering trees, walking trails, shrubs, plants, flowers and an overwhelming sense of peace at the Garden of Gethsemane. It is amazing.

Adam and Eve walked with God in a garden.

Jesus had an appointment in this same garden.

We were instructed to branch out, move around, and find a secluded spot on our own to sit and meditate, to talk to God, be still or whatever our spirits and souls needed to do in the garden.

I chose a large stone just off the pathway to sit on. I looked to the left and to the right, no one. My stone was under a large tree, with a grassy area just across from me. I sat upon my stone and listened. The garden was so quiet and except for the occasional bird call it was still.

From my vantagepoint I looked out across the Kidron Valley up towards the Dome of the Rock and the outer temple walls. I looked out over thousands and thousands of burial tombs but that did not bother me. The garden was breath taking.

Part way through our meditation time, a large, obnoxious sound blared out from a loudspeaker just across the way from me. It was the call to prayer for the Muslims. It startled the silence, broke through my mind and became a distraction that was not easily ignored. The horn blared out it's instructions and ancient music just as it has for thousands of years. It was my first time hearing the call to prayer and I marveled at the obnoxious loudness of the sound.

I looked up the path and saw a person coming towards me from our group, not sure why they were wandering around as we were supposed to be sitting still in one spot, having alone time with God. It bothered me, this person came closer and closer and then took a picture of me. By now I was annoyed at the blaring sound, and now annoyed at this person and then I heard the word: Distraction.

Gardens, a place to enjoy, serenity, peaceful but they are full of distractions.

Gardens have bugs, weeds, plants to care for, trim or tie up, fruit to be picked, gardens have distractions.

Adam and Eve had a serpent.

Jesus had torture and suffering.

Mine had strangers, and obnoxious noises.

God was giving me my first lesson, of many, on distractions. I was there in the garden to be with Him, spend quality time and instead I was fussing and fuming over all the other things in the garden.

He used the distraction analogy many times in Israel, letting me know that distractions in life are many and unless we fight against them, they will steal our time with God.

How do we stop distractions?

This lesson has continued here in Canada since my trip to Israel. I often here that still voice whisper "distraction".

I want to share a blog written by my youngest son on Distractions:

_____

"Life is full of distractions. You must be careful which voices you listen to or allow yourself to be influenced by. It seems that everywhere you look there are people, or ads or pictures or videos telling you how to live, what to eat, what to wear, what your body should look like, where you should live, what you should drive, where you should work... you get the point.
It's so easy to get distracted by these other voices or what's going on around you, that you might forget just where it was you were heading to. Like a drunk person staggering down the road from the bar after a

night out, you might stumble if you allow yourself to listen to these voices.

That's why we must be careful what we allow ourselves to hear. We must put God's voice above all. Above your wife or husband or your kids (I know pretty easy to say when you're a bachelor with no kids). Above your family, your friends, your boss. You must listen carefully to what the Spirit is saying.

The enemy is always lurking in the shadows, peering around the corner, waiting to put his foot out and make you fall. He wants you to fall face first without any warning.

Things in life have come up and they seem to have me veering off track from Gods plan. When I say I've been distracted, I mean I've been allowing other things to influence me in a way that blocks me from hearing Gods voice. I didn't do it on purpose, but it still happened.

This week I planned a fast and I did manage to make it three days. Not the seven days I'd said I was going to do but still an all time high for myself. When I finished my fast, I'd been feeling a bit down. I didn't notice a difference, other than some events that happened during the week that really distracted me even more. I went to prayer night at church and could definitely feel Gods presence in a big way, I also did have a vision of an eagle and also flock of sheep come to me at the end of prayer, which was quite interesting.

After prayer was prophesy night, we learned about the gift of discernment, also talked about hearing Gods voice and recognizing it as Gods voice. There are four spiritual places we can hear voices coming from. Your own spirit tells you things, demonic spirits, angelic spirits as well as Gods Holy Spirit.

When we are listening or doing something that we think is being spoken to us by God. It is important we know that is exactly where it is coming from. I find myself confused a lot of the time lately because I think I am being led by the Holy Spirit, but soon find out I was not. I then get frustrated and I tend to run away from my problems, when I do this I also tend push God away at the same time.

Well last night God said STOP RUNNING. I didn't recognize this message as being for myself, I thought I was supposed to give someone else this word actually. After distracting myself with thoughts of running far away, I decided to go for a walk. This is where I really heard God speak to me again. There was a person walking in front of me on my usual trail and I was trying to clear my head with nobody around. I happened to notice a trail in the trees that must've been a game trail. This trail led me to an embankment, it paralleled along a steep edge for few feet. I stopped right in the middle of the part that was on top of the bank and heard God speak. He said "Ray you are so close, you're almost there, you're standing on the edge and I need you to take a leap into my arms."

I am constantly trying to control things in my life, I have yet to allow God to take full control of the wheel. God needs to guide us completely, if we are going to follow him, there's no in between. You're either letting him drive or you're not. God has asked me to take this leap and that's just what I plan to do.

It's easier to say it than it is to do it. We are all human and it is uncomfortable to allow things to spiral out of our control. We need to recognize that when this happens, our life isn't spiraling out of control. Our life is actually being shaped into what it is supposed to be. God is

molding us into who he intended us to be and this may not feel good at the time, so I've learned, but the end result will be better than we can even imagine. Before you can be comfortable, you're going to need to be uncomfortable first. Whatever it is that God has put on your heart to do, I'm sure there is something, you should probably tune into that. You will first need to step off of that ledge though. It's not going to be comforting at first, but God is there to catch you."
By Ray Baker

Matthew 6:34 NLT "So don't worry about tomorrow, for tomorrow will bring it's own worries. Today's trouble is enough for today."

1 Timothy 6:12 NLT "Fight the good fight for the true faith. Hold tightly to the eternal life to which God has called you, which you have confessed so well before many witnesses."[2]

I think Ray has captured the essence of distractions perfectly in his blog. There were distractions in Israel, there are distractions at home.

Distractions come at you wherever you are in the world, wherever you are in your walk with God. Learning to hear and heed the voice of God is the only way we can hope to differentiate the call of God and the distraction. They can both seem to lead to good places, or to the edge of a cliff. In one case you jump and hope for mercy and in the other you jump but only into the hand of God, a safe landing.

---

[2] © Ray Baker, 2019 Published on Midweek Moments October 9, 2019

Distractions were something I fought hugely in Israel, the land of many cultures and spirits and I continue to fight them at home, where something is always vying for my attention.

Notes & Nuggets:

Notes & Nuggets:

CHAPTER 7

THE ENEMIES

While I was in Israel, I had an encounter for the entire time I was there with a woman who followed me around, quite literally. She had a background with satanic ritual abuse as sadly she had been born into that lifestyle.

By day eight, I started to get really unnerved by her and became almost fearful with her showing up beside me or following me around. She was a part of our "group" but for some reason she was attached to me. It was not only myself that noticed it, my roommate as well. I ended up talking to Sarah, my leader, about it and she offered some great advice, but cautioned me that I was on the top of

Mount Carmel where the biggest spiritual battle of all time had occurred – what did I think would happen when I went there?

Good point! I was in a very real spiritual battle, this one simply had flesh on.

I prayed, covered myself with God's protection every day, verbally and mentally put on the full armor of God Ephesians 6:8-10 daily. Still this woman would not let up. She brought a spirit of confusion with her wherever she went and totally caused confusion in a workshop on prayer to the point several people left, and some were crying. It was interesting to watch her in action but not so interesting to be followed.

Simcha, another one of my leaders told me that the above daily "provisions" of praying, covering myself with God's protection, and putting on the armor were a great start but that we are at war, so now what is my strategy?

She said that if I had been doing all of the above things back at home and then going about my day, going to work or to the grocery store , they were good for back then, but this is now, we are at war, what is my now strategy?

I answered weakly, "strategy?"

She said, "Yes. When a country goes to war, they have a room, a command center and they meet and they make plans, they strategize, they cast vision and lead."

She said, "it would be a little late to make the strategy after the war was over."

This is a key piece of advice for the days we live in.

I spent time in prayer asking God what my "strategy" should be. He gave me a couple of great ideas and I did them. I was feeling pretty good on the last day of our trip when we all got together and of course this lady was in our little group with me. We closed our session by praying for each other.

When it was my turn, I was seated in a chair in the middle and the group gathered around to pray for me. The very first person to pray for me and put her hand right onto the middle of my back, while my head was down and my eyes were closed, was this woman. I thought nothing of it at the time.

Afterward she got me alone and said to me, "you are a mighty woman of God."

A couple of days before, I might not have been able to answer the way I did as I had been caving in to some "fear" but now I had worked it through so I turned to her and said, "Yes I am."

She went on, "I see you going out with your sword and taking down the enemy and you have a long line of carnage behind you. But if I was you, I would taper it down a bit."

Every ounce of me rose up and I replied, "I don't think so".

She gave me a smile and moved on.

It was not until after our move in our new house three months later when I crashed emotionally, physically and spiritually to the point where I scared myself. I met with a lady who I trust with Godly discernment to the upmost.

She told me that God was not letting her have any peace about my "exhaustion". She could not explain it and she had been praying for me a lot, but she told me that what kept coming to her was this lady in Israel. She went on to ask me, "did she by any chance, at any time happen to...."

"Touch me?" I finished her sentence myself. I looked at her and nodded.

She said, "I thought so. I think you have picked up a spirit from this lady in Israel, I'm sorry."

There was nothing for her to be sorry about, as she said it, I felt it was truth, but I waited until two other people confirmed it for me.

Things inside my body had started to go quite wonky. My eyes blurred, my head hurt, not like a headache but an actual pain, I at times lost my words, my thinking got confused, I was soooo tired, I was dizzy and I kept tripping like something was pushing me or tripping me. I felt like I was being attacked from the inside out. I did not trust myself to talk or speak, I was not sure I should be driving (as one time I could not figure out that the car was still moving when I was trying to open the car door to get out). I was scary. I started to stay home as much as I could and not talk to people, as I was not sure I could hold a conversation.

I have done deliverance ministry, that is where someone tells the unwanted spirits to get the heck out of your body. I tried to do it for myself. I had a couple of friends pray for me and anoint me with oil. I was only getting worse. What I was doing was not working.

I called the church to see if the Pastors could pray for me. Before I went to Israel, I felt that I needed to get the Blessing from the Pastors to go and I felt that this "thing" needed the Pastors to pray to tell it to go. The Pastors were all away. I asked if there were Elders available to pray.

In the New Testament Jesus addresses different spirits in different ways as there are many different kinds of spirits.

The disciples were not able to cast some spirits out. Matthew 17:19-20 (lack of faith)

Mark 9:28-29 (this kind can only come out by prayer)

I have learned by working with people and spirits, that different spirits have different jobs and different levels of authority and quite frankly sometimes it takes someone with more authority than you to remove certain spirits.

Similar to a hockey or football team, there are lead players and the rest of the team – you cannot play with just the lead players, you need back up and reinforcements – this is how the spiritual world works as well. When you get a "quarterback" sometimes you need to call in the coach to deal with it and a person with a "quarterback" usually has a whole team participating.

I had asked God what the name of this particular spirit was. When you ask spirits their name or ask God to reveal their name, they will.

Matthew 5:9
"Then Jesus asked him, "What is your name?"
"My name is Legion," he replied, "for we are many.

Turns out mine was called: destruction.

Upon getting the name, I drove immediately to the church and blurted out this whole story as best I could, trying to find and connect words and hold it together. I guess I looked the part as both at work and the church staff all commented on how awful I looked. I had three Elders and one very discerning friend come that very night to pray for me.

To make a long story shorter, I will highlight the prayer session, which was amazing!

- One Elder said that he felt like even though this spirit was in me, that this was now a "body" thing. Now that the story was out, that this now was a matter for the church body, it belonged to "us". That was such a powerful statement. The Bible states that we are all different but all one body, when one part suffers the whole body suffers.

"If one part suffers, every part suffers with it; if one part is honored, every part rejoices with it." 1 Corinthians 12:26

When he said those words, a huge and very sweet sense of peace and calm filled the room. This was a statement of "authority".

- We, as a group, stood on the Word of God and told with scripture (authority) this spirit in no uncertain terms that it had no legal ground to be there and that it needed to leave me and the premises.

- Someone saw in a vision an arrow in my back and that they saw Jesus come and pull it out.

Now just before that was said, I had the most unusual sensation in my back. It felt like a suction cup had been pulled out. At that very moment I knew beyond a doubt that whatever had been put onto /into me was now gone. Jesus had indeed come and pulled the arrow (spiritual) out of my back.

I started to feel joy, I prayed with passion, I wanted to sing – I Was Free! Praise God for His faithfulness!

An arrow in my back – I have thought about that a lot. That would be a slow bleed, a slow death. It had started in Israel unbeknown to me and by that last week I looked and felt so horrible I knew something major was wrong, destruction was trying to take its place.

Why do I share this story with you? For sensationalism? Hardly! I did not want to share it in the first place, and I struggle as I write it to even share it. I do not want to frighten people, but it is a real and very important part of this life we live. It is not a subject we hear talked about much anywhere, short of tv shows and movies that dwell on the dark spiritual side and are top box-office money-making productions. The world is drawn to it but the church backs away.

I know many of the things that come at us in life are not in the natural, they are in the spiritual and sometimes we try to make sense out of something that is not sensible or logical. The spirit world is not logical.

Spiritual attachments to us personally and even down our family generations are called "familiar" spirits. They wreak havoc on our health, our emotions, our behavior and almost anything they can get attached to.

There is a train of thought in some of our Christian churches that once you are a Christian, satan cannot touch you. This is a thought that comes right from the pit of hell, of course satan would love for you to believe that. I have worked with many believing Christians that have struggled with some form of spiritual attacks and demons.

Let's mention a couple of things that negate this line of thinking:

<u>Jesus, the sinless one</u>: satan came to Him and tempted Him face to face.

<u>Job:</u> satan was allowed to totally assault the man and his family.

Job 1: 6-7 "One day the angels came to present themselves before the Lord, and Satan also came with them. ⁷ The Lord said to Satan, "Where have you come from?"
Satan answered the Lord, "From roaming throughout the earth, going back and forth on it."
Job 2:1-2 "On another day the angels came to present themselves before the Lord, and Satan also came with them to present himself before him. ² And the Lord said to Satan, "Where have you come from?"
Satan answered the Lord, "From roaming throughout the earth, going back and forth on it."

Zechariah 3:1 "Then he showed me Joshua the high priest standing before the angel of the LORD, and Satan standing at his right side to accuse him."

---

11 of the 12 disciples were martyred for their faith, a destruction spirit was definitely at work here trying to wipe followers of Jesus off the map.

Judas – the betrayer of Jesus. The scripture says, satan entered into Judas. Luke 22:3, John 13:27

Romans: 8:38-39 "For I am persuaded, that neither death, nor life, nor angels, nor principalities, nor powers, nor things present, nor things to come. Nor height, nor depth, nor any other creature, shall be able to separate us from the love of God, which is in Christ Jesus our Lord."

The above scripture states that nothing can separate us from the love of God and it lists the things that will try: angels, principalities (satan has a principality), powers (satan has powers), any creature (satan is a created creature)

My friends, we are at war, and this war rages 24 hours a day 7 days a week. We give God ten minutes of our day and think that will withstand the onslaught. Satan would like nothing better that to get his grip on and into your life and your family, your country and do some collateral damage and guess what? **He strategizes** to get maximum impact and damage.

A couple of very important questions:

1) Do you know for a fact that the Holy Spirit of God, the third person of the Trinity, lives within you?

You have to ask Him to come and live inside you.

This is so important; I am sure it was only the power of the Holy Spirit that kept me going for those weeks home. The power of God living within you is, quite frankly, Amazing!

2) What is your strategy?

We, you and I are at war with an enemy of our souls and fighting for our families. He is cagey, sneaky and vicious, guard your body, spirit, soul and minds with great diligence. Know your Bible, the Word of God is a powerful weapon. At the name of Jesus all spirits will bow.

Sing out your song, use your musical weapon. Praise has the power to crush and smash demonic strongholds.

3) Please consider when people want to lay hands on you, do you know them/ trust them?

It may be unwise. Transference of spirits can happen through the touch of human hands from one person to another. I'm not talking about a hug, but a laying on of hands in prayer.

4) Do you have a group where you belong to the "body"?

I had never met two of the three Elders who prayed for me, but we were on common ground because we knew what each other believed being at the same church. The meeting that night was such a sweet time of bonding, power and unity.

We need each other. When one member of the body suffers, the whole body suffers. I am so thankful that I had a body behind me that was able to stand with me in the fight.

This is never more evident than in Israel. This small bit of land that is the most fought over, contested and struggling for existence. Just as you and I need the body, they also need us to pray and contend for them. Israel is the pinnacle of Gods time clock. **We are commanded to pray for the peace of Israel, for Jerusalem.** Psalm 83 & 122:6

The Bible says it will bless those who pray and are kind to Israel. Do you want God's blessing? Pray for Israel.

If you do not believe me that we, you and I and our countries including Israel, need other members of a believing body, use the following analogy about your human body.

Stub your toe, sprain your ankle, break a bone, and then tell the rest of your body it's no big deal and to get over it! One injury can bring your entire body to a standstill remarkably fast in both the human body and the church body.

We need each other!

Notes & Nuggets:

Notes & Nuggets:

CHAPTER 8

THE ISAIAH 19 HIGHWAY

I have to admit that when I learned I was going to Israel, fear crept in. Israel, just the word in our North American culture brings images of war, devastation, anxiety and unrest.

I was torn about going at first because of the war talk and rumors of wars. While in Israel they talk openly about the possibility of war. For the people of Israel, it is no big deal. The Jewish people have been at war with one country or another for thousands of years. All the people I met have many stories of running to the bomb shelter, it is common there, it is life. They are not scared of war; they are living in and under the threat of it daily.

I, personally, found Israel to be a country of incredible peace, contentment and joy regardless of the threat from outside.

As we look around us, the prophecies of the Bible are speeding up and coming true.

One of the terms that I heard a lot in Israel, that I have never heard in North America, is the One New Man teaching. The One New Man in Israel is Messianic Jews, Gentiles and Arabs all believing together. There are numerous believers coming to faith all over the Middle East and in Egypt.

Isaiah 19: 23-25 is a banner verse for the One New Man teaching.

"In that day there will be a highway from Egypt to Assyria. The Assyrians will go to Egypt and the Egyptians to Assyria. The Egyptians and Assyrians will worship together. In that day Israel will be the third, along with Egypt and Assyria, a blessing] on the earth. The LORD Almighty will bless them, saying, "Blessed be Egypt my people, Assyria my handiwork, and Israel my inheritance."

The covenant promise that God made to Abraham where the earth would be blessed through him back in Genesis 12:1-3 is now coming true in the Isaiah 19 highway.

If you drew a line up from Egypt up to Iran, Turkey, the highway would run right through Jerusalem. Jerusalem is God's Holy City. The Bride of Christ is the new city of Jerusalem. (Revelation 21: 2) Jesus spilled His blood right in the middle of the Isaiah 19 highway. He died for people of all nations and countries.

John witnessed and was told in Revelation 21:2, that of "the holy city, new Jerusalem, coming down from God out of heaven, prepared as a bride adorned for her husband".

The beginning of the church began with a handful of faithful Jewish believers who went out into the world at God's direction and brought the gospel to the whole world. When Jesus comes back it will be the same, we will be worshipping together as one new man.

The Isaiah 19 highway can only happen through Jesus. Gentile believers, Jewish believers, Arab believers become family together in unity.

"In that day...." this is how the Isaiah 19 verse starts. What day? When?

Many in Israel and around the middle east, believe that day is now. This highway has been started in the spiritual realm. It is not a physical highway, but a spiritual one that takes territory for God in the Middle East.

I was able to hear stories of what is happening in the Middle East while I was in Israel, I heard firsthand reports of incredible things that God is doing.

An estimated 1.2 million Iraqis were displaced in 2014. Over 1.1 million Syrian refugees are registered and living in camps in Lebanon. The conditions in the refugee camps is atrocious for all these people and many of them are children.

God has been moving in the midst of these hurting, displaced people. I heard a report that there are reportedly 7-8 million believers in Iran. They are not allowed to openly worship as it is a Muslim country, so they meet in house churches. One man was in charge of over 400 house churches, the leaders of most of the churches were all in their early 20's.

We need to pray and support organizations doing work over there, the house church leaders are leading but need discipling, they need resources, believing mentors. The people in the camps need basic humanitarian necessities.

Highway 19 Ministries is one of the organizations working in the refugee camps, they believe people of the earth will be blessed because of Abraham. Much of the help for the refugees is coming out of Israel and other God believing organizations.

Here is an excerpt from their website:

"Derech Avraham is Hebrew for "the way of Abraham". Derech Avraham is a kingdom initiative that is not exclusive to one organization or ministry alone. It is a partnership in a shared vision, supported and staffed by a unified team of leaders serving in various capacities in the Middle East.

The convergence of the missions movement, prayer movement and church planting & discipleship movements is providing multi-faceted opportunities for ministry in the Middle East. Derech Avraham embraces the graces and values of each of these streams in it's mobilizing, equipping and deployment strategies.

A relational network of Middle Eastern nationals and internationals working in various spheres of ministry with a kingdom vision of the Middle East that is best outlined in Isaiah's vision of a highway in Isaiah 19:23-25 Our goal is to facilitate a reunion of Isaac & Ishmael – the nations of the Middle East – that will build a highway to bless the nations."

Is that not incredible! God's promises are coming true, in our day!

You see people cannot meet God and stay the same, it is impossible. Everyone who has met with God knows that their future will be different than their past. We are God's hands and feet and our job while meeting the physical needs of the people is to share with them their biggest need, the spiritual one: Introduce them to Jesus. It is happening all over the Middle East and along the Silk Road.

For everything that God does, satan has a counterfeit. God's Plan A. is for the people of the earth to come together in unity, One New Man.

Could it be that satan's counterfeit, Plan B, is the One World Order? This movement of one government, one currency, one religion: a total opposite of the One New Man. The One World Order looks similar and sounds like a logical plan, however it is a system that is designed to control, put in place by rulers. It is not a system designed for freedom and unity like God's plan, the One New Man.

The Messianic Church that I was privileged to be a part of for ten days, started the first Drug and Alcohol Rehab center in Israel where Jew and Arab were encouraged to live life together joining the two as One New Man. This was taboo by both Arabs and Jews.

They also have a housing and ministry project for widows and children from Northern Africa. They house them and teach them life and job skills so they could learn to support themselves. I got to meet some of these amazing people who had been rescued by the saving work of Jesus through the Messianic church.

I heard firsthand reports that the number of Christians in Egypt is increasing daily.

One gentleman that came to talk to us, a Pastor, was on a plane a couple years ago and an East Indian man from India was seated next to him. He asked the man what he did for a living and the East Indian gentleman said he was a Pastor. Intrigued over this since India is not known as a Christian nation, he asked him, how big a church he pastored.

The East Indian Pastor replied, "20,000".

Wow! God is at work, even when we cannot see it. God is at work because He said He would Bless all the nations of the earth through Abraham.

We need to understand the importance of Declaring and Proclaiming God's Prophecies and Promises over the land.

This is another of the keys to God's Kingdom.

We, as a team, went about many places in Israel praying and proclaiming the ground for God. God is raising up governmental intercessors, people who will pray and proclaim for the governments, because with God all things are possible. With prayer and proclamation, we can change governments, policies and the future.

"If my people, which are called by my name, shall humble themselves, and pray, and seek my face, and turn from their wicked ways; then will I hear from heaven, and will forgive their sin, and will heal their land." 2 Chronicles 7:14
"Then the Lord reached out his hand and touched my mouth and said to me, "I have put my words in your mouth. See, today I appoint you

over nations and kingdoms to uproot and tear down, to destroy and overthrow, to build and to plant." Jeremiah 1:9-10

One man told us the story that God had told him a few years ago that He was going to start building the Isaiah 19 Highway. This man was told to go to three cities north of Israel and pray and declare over them God's promises and Blessings. One of the cities was Baghdad, where is it very dangerous to be a believer.

He went, out of obedience, to the cities and walked and prayed over them, making God's prophetic declarations over the land and territories. He went for breakfast in Baghdad to a restaurant, only men could eat there. He got into a conversation with another man. This other fellow was from Egypt, they got to feeling the ground out carefully in conversation, but went on to discover that God had told both of these men, both Pastors to go to the same three cities and make prayerful declarations over the territory. They could not have possibly known that God was working and telling the same message to others along the Isaiah 19 highway route, but what a confirmation that God would let these two men find each other.

The God of the Extravagant is working all around the world!
It is up to us to claim ground, declare and proclaim God's promises over your land, your city, your country and around the world.

Notes & Nuggets:

Notes & Nuggets:

CHAPTER 9

ON THE OUTSIDE LOOKING IN

B efore I went to Israel my group leaders asked me why I wanted to go. I replied that I believed that I settled for crumbs from God and I wanted to experience the God of extravagance. I wanted God's dump truck. I had many impactful lessons in Israel, but the following one actually moved my heart, mind and soul.

It was a picture, no, a mural, painted bigger than life on the side wall of a little cathedral in a church on the shores of the Sea of Galilee in the town that was Magdala.

You walked into a circular room, with stone bench seats all around the exterior on the walls. The middle of the room was empty save a marble slab for a podium and this amazing painting staring down at you. I could not take my eyes off the painting. The feelings it stirred up in me were unfamiliar but yet not.

The picture depicts the story of the Woman with the Issue of Blood from the Bible told in Luke 8:43-48, Matthew 9:20-22 and Mark 5:24-35 (NIV New International Version)

"A large crowd followed and pressed around him. And a woman was there who had been subject to bleeding for twelve years. She had suffered a great deal under the care of many doctors and had spent all she had, yet instead of getting better she grew worse. When she heard about Jesus, she came up behind him in the crowd and touched his cloak, because she thought, "If I just touch his clothes, I will be healed." Immediately her bleeding stopped, and she felt in her body that she was freed from her suffering.

At once Jesus realized that power had gone out from him. He turned around in the crowd and asked, "Who touched my clothes?"

"You see the people crowding against you," his disciples answered, "and yet you can ask, 'Who touched me?'"

But Jesus kept looking around to see who had done it. Then the woman, knowing what had happened to her, came and fell at his feet and, trembling with fear, told him the whole truth.

He said to her, "Daughter, your faith has healed you. Go in peace and be freed from your suffering." Mark 5:24-35

I prayed and asked God why this picture was affecting me so. What came to me was a surprise.

I was on the outside looking in, I was not in Jesus' inner circle, therefore the woman in the picture could have been me.

I wondered what this exactly meant for me. Apparently, I spend my time with God watching and waiting for Him to move and then I join Him. I am not in the inner circle, like the staff room or at the water cooler or in the disciple's circle where they sit around and talk about the day, their life, their comings and goings. I choose to rather sit apart and watch, on the outside looking in. Sadly, I identified and recognized this statement to be very true of me.

This woman had been sick for twelve years and she had spent all she had trying to be healed. That means she had spent herself financially, but also emotionally, and spiritually for she had "suffered much."

I am sure she could not have counted the number of times she had cried out to God to heal her. She was a Jewish woman, she knew about God, she had been taught about prayer and sacrifices. I wonder how many sacrifices she had bought and took to the priests to offer up, to pay for her sins – real or imagined. Since God had not healed her, she must have thought she was guilty of something very large.

This woman had to call out in a loud voice "unclean, unclean" everywhere she went, warning people that if they touched her, they too would become "unclean". People cleared a path or scurried out of the way whenever she called out. The loneliness and barrenness of her life was a large vacuum of isolation and heartbreak.

I remember a time where I too had an issue of blood for over three years, it almost killed me, literally. It was debilitating. It stole from me, taking my life, my pride, my body, my energy, my "normalness". I went from doctor to doctor to try to seek a cure, a miracle, a solution. It took three years before I got surgery to fix my issue. For this woman surgery was not even an option.

She was desperate and if I might add, totally a Jane add, she probably wished she were dead on more than one occasion.

This woman had tried everything she had heard of to be healed and then she heard that Jesus was coming. She had heard rumors and stories that Jesus healed. She wondered if He had healing for her too and she found a boldness to try to venture near enough to touch Him.

To do this she needed to be silent, to not cry out "unclean", she made up her mind to love herself more than others. She had to break the law, she had to deceive the crowds that were swarming around Jesus, jostling and pushing all trying just to be near Him. She knew that because she was "unclean" she did not stand a chance to physically stand in Jesus presence; no one wanted her near.

Somehow this woman knew if she could just "touch the hem of His garment" that she would be healed. How did she know that? How could she possibly get near to Jesus, who had hundreds of people vying for His attention?

Like this woman, a person who is on the outside looking in, watches, contemplates, listens, they learn by watching. Call it people watching or whatever name you want, but people watchers figure out people.

This woman had years of watching, waiting and listening. No one talked to her, she had no chance of family or friends anymore, she lived by herself, alone. She was always off from the crowds, never included, she was always on the outside looking in. She had heard that Jesus was going through her town, it would be a one-time only event, a one-time chance at being healed.

It had been a long twelve years and she wanted, no she needed, a chance to live.

She deliberately had to set her face like flint and make the decision to touch Jesus. Men and women were never to touch in that culture, this was a gutsy woman or perhaps desperate times called for more desperate measures.

I have read this story many, many times, but I do not think that I pictured this woman crawling through the legs of walking people, crawling through the dirt, the muck and mire laying on the roadways.

I find it interesting that this woman had to go face first to the ground in a crawling position, a position of worship, a posture of submission.

How did she not trip the walkers? She had to crawl or crouch down, get low and figure out which legs were Jesus'? Which sandals were His? Which were His toes? Which robe was the one to touch? She had only moments, not minutes to reach out and touch the fabric before she would be exposed.

Imagine her surprise when she did reach out and touch the right fabric, the right hem and she could feel in her body a difference. What was she feeling? Elation? Surprise? Excitement? And then she heard those dreaded words…. "who touched Me?"

Stunned, she knew she was caught, there would be no escape.

Picture her straightening up, humiliated and knowing there would be punishment, head bent low for she could not look Jesus in the eye or anyone else for that matter. She heard the gasps as the town people recognized her as the "unclean" woman, the untouchable one. She felt their contempt and scorn as their steely eyes drilled into her soul, she could feel their accusations and so caught, she confesses what she has done. She hears the scuffling of the feet as the crowd parts rapidly, backing away from her, retreating further and further away as they realize they cannot touch her, that she is still the "unclean" one.

Then the voice, that voice, the voice of Jesus speaks, not accusingly, not forcefully, but gently and kindly, the voice is directed to her. "Daughter" – how long has it been since anyone, said a kind word to her? How long has it been since anyone included her into their family and now Jesus is saying "daughter" – a daughter of Abraham, including her into her Jewish family.

Astounded now and in wonder she raises her head to look up into the face of Jesus. He continues... "your faith has healed you. Go in peace and be freed from your suffering."

Jesus never chastises her, there is no punishment, rather there is praise for her faith, there is freedom and healing – life awaits her!

This woman believed that touching Jesus hem would heal her, this little act of touching His hem, brought about a life changing miracle.

God talked to me that day about living on the outside, that I was believing that the scraps, the crumbs, "the hem" were enough.

Why did I believe I was created for the outside? Why was I happy with being on the outside? Why could I not believe that Jesus Himself wanted me in the inner circle?

I realize that many of us, not just myself, are content to live on the outside.

He brought to my mind that I believed I was not good enough to be inside the circle and by believing that lie, that I was shortchanging myself and God all at the same time. I, me, had prevented Him from being God of the Extravagant.

He does not want us to settle for the hem, to settle for little touches when He has big miracles, big lessons and so much more life to give us.

I went to Israel to discover the God of the extravagant and by showing me this mural, He made me realize I did not think I deserved more than the hem. God showed up with His dump truck regularly, but I could never see it, because I was on the outside looking in.

That woman was not content to live on the outside any longer, she was desperate for more.

What about me? Am I content or am I desperate enough to want more?

What about you?

Notes & Nuggets:

Notes & Nuggets:

CHAPTER 10

FAITH

W repeat this Bible verse a lot: faith as small as a mustard seed.

---

*Jesus says, "The kingdom of heaven is like to a grain of **mustard seed**, which is the **smallest** of all **seeds** on earth. Yet when planted, it grows and becomes the largest of all garden plants, with such big branches that the birds can perch in its shade." Mark 4:30-32*

"He replied, "Because you have so little faith. Truly I tell you, if you have faith as small as a mustard seed, you can say to this mountain, 'Move from here to there,' and it will move. Nothing will be impossible for you." Matthew 17:20, Luke 17:6,

---

Well I have now seen a mustard flower and mustard seed and I can tell you; both are little.
The mustard flower is a bright yellow flower that grows all over in Israel, to me it looked like a North American Buttercup.

The seed in the flower is so small it is barely there, that is how small your faith can be: barely there.

I kind of think that might have been what Jesus was implying here. My faith is barely there and that is because I am a human. God, through His Holy Spirit gives us faith as He lives inside of us.

If I pray and pray and pray for something and it does not happen, then the ramifications of what did not happen fall onto me. I live with the shame that I did not have enough faith, to make something happen. This is a despicable lie that has been given to so many sick people, hurting people, making them think they are to blame for their lack of faith.

Reality is, I can make NOTHING happen. Only God can.

God's reality is not ours and ours is not Gods. We can no more "WISH" our prayers onto God and "make Him do something" by doing earnest prayer than we can do time travel. It will not work.
I would interpret the mustard seed verses more like: "if I believe in God and in His power, then all things are possible if God decides to do them."

This is so much different than, "if I pray and pray and pray and beg God, He will do it my way." It really does not happen that way.

One of our teachers in Israel said it this way: if you want an answer to prayer then ask a little old believing lady to pray or go into your house, close the door, draw a circle on the floor, step into the circle and pray intensely for everyone standing inside the circle.

God will change the world as we change, as we surrender as we become more like Jesus.

Does this mean we should not pray for others? Heck no!

Prayer is one of the kingdom keys God works on the earth. It is vital.

A person is powerless in the kingdom of God if he is prayerless. Your private prayer life is the one that counts, not the public one. Private prayer equals power in the kingdom.

Elijah prayed that it would not rain, and it did not rain again until he prayed for it to, years later.

"Now Elijah the Tishbite was a prophet from the settlers in Gilead. "I serve the Lord, the God of Israel," Elijah said to Ahab. "As surely as the Lord lives, no rain or dew will fall during the next few years unless I command it." 1 Kings 17

Elijah had a powerful ministry, but he also had a powerful relationship with his God. He was a friend of God, God and Elijah communicated together, they had relationship. Relationship with God equals spiritual clearness and power.

I have yet to decide who is my favorite in the Bible, Elijah or Job. These were men of impeccable spiritual and physical power, whom God counted as His friends. People noticed there was something different about them. Satan took notice of Job as well and he suffered greatly at his hand, although God restored Job in the end.

Elijah, the brave and mighty man of God, had a hiccup in his life named Jezebel. This woman put fear deep into the heart of Elijah and he turned and ran.

What was it about Jezebel that scared him so much?

Jezebel was a powerful and wicked woman; her goal was to destroy or stop the work of God. She challenged the status quo of God's work. She was self-seeking and operated out of a spirit of envy; very much like satan she wished to be in control of all of God's kingdom.

She called herself a prophetess, taught and seduced people to her way of thinking. Jezebel had a weak husband, Ahab, that she could control. Jezebel wore the pants in her home.

There is a huge increase in the world today of the spirit of Jezebel. It will usually be in a woman, often with a weak husband or no husband at all. She will appear very religious, often the first one to cry and will volunteer or work in the church with the intent to challenge and thwart God's purposes.

The church will cease to grow outward if Jezebel is in control, it will start to only look at itself. Jezebel will have a following of "yes men/women" who she has convinced to follow and go to her instead of God, she rules by fear and intimidation. The Jezebel spirit will not be accountable to others, she will not be teachable. The ultimate passion of a Jezebel is control and her direct attack is at God's leaders.

The Jezebel spirit mimics the prophetic gift of God but is a counterfeit. People will be drawn in because the spiritual will seem to be so "real/true" of a Jezebel. Satan always takes the truth and twists it slightly, so it is hard to decern the real from the false without Holy Spirit discernment.

This particular spirit releases confusion has a critical spirit and wants decision making authority.

How does a Jezebel spirit get a foothold? A woman leader who seeks control over all areas in a church or ministry is a prime candidate for satan to tempt to want to have it all. Greed, pride and selfishness is at the root.

You will have noticed that women have been elevated in the media, tv, movies to now be the bosses, the champions and the heroes, usurping the men. This is prime conditioning for the spirit of Jezebel.

Society has been set up to receive the super women into their midst, she simply walks in.

In Israel, one of the pastors had a woman come into his church with the spirit of Jezebel and she prayed for the pastor and laid hands on him. She passed onto him a spirit of infirmity, he had to go and have it removed after he got so sick. Jezebel wants to cripple the church and take over.

Personally, in my life I know a few of these women. I believe I met one of them in Israel, the woman who followed me. I have asked God what I am to do with this information about the Jezebel spirit, and He has told me that it is not my fight, it is His. It is a spiritual battle between God and satan. My assignment is to pray that her work would not damage the church or the people in the church. Prayer is the war cry against Jezebel.

In Elijah's day it was not Elijah who took down Jezebel, rather God sent someone specifically with the assignment to take down Jezebel and her kingdom. She was killed and her body was eaten by stray dogs, just as the true prophet of God, Elijah had predicted.

The Spirit of Elijah has also been released on the world today. The Spirit of Elijah is a spirit ready to go and make the people ready for the spirit of the Lord. This is a spirit that is not self-seeking, it is a spirit of surrender to God.

The good Samaritan had an Elijah spirit, seeking to pour himself out for others. The Spirit of Elijah will turn back the hearts of fathers to their children, we live in such a fatherless society, we need our men more than ever. Elijah spent a couple of years with a widow and her son, pouring himself into the life of this little boy as a surrogate father. The Spirit of Elijah is the spirit of Jesus and the world is ready to see and hear the good news.

Will you be one of the faithful to go and preach to your family, your friends, your neighbors, your co-workers? Will you serve them out of love just like Jesus would have?

Notes & Nuggets:

Notes & Nuggets:

CHAPTER 11

THE SIGNIFICANCE

The question that hovers over and around Israel is, what, if any, is the significance of this little tiny country? In the grand scheme of worldwide things, does Israel, and what happens in it, or to it, have any bearing on my own life or the plans of the world?

The answer to both of these questions is a resounding: **YES.**

"Now the Lord had said unto Abram, Get thee out of thy country, and from thy kindred, and from thy father's house, unto a land that I will shew thee: And I will make of thee a great nation, and I will bless thee, and make thy name great; and thou shalt be a blessing: And I will

bless them that bless thee, and curse him that curseth thee: and in thee shall all families of the earth be blessed." Genesis 12:1–3

"I will Bless them that Bless Israel and I will Curse Those who Curse Israel and in thee, ALL the families of the earth will be blessed." This promise spoken by God to Abraham. Abraham did not have to be good, he did not have to perform, or do anything to have this promise spoken over him. God chose Abraham and declared it to be so and it will be, and only will be because God said so.

That is a very large and powerful promise made by the Creator of the Universe to Abraham. Through Abraham, for no apparent reason that depended on Abraham, all the families of the earth would be blessed. Blessings and curses for each one of us are also dependent on our attitude, prayers and support of the country of Israel and the people of Israel.

Yes, the significance of Israel is monstrously huge in the grand scheme of things in the world.

Israel is the tiny country that did not choose to be chosen. God chose the Israeli people to become His people not because of who they were, but simply because He chose them.

Anyone who touches Israel will have to contend with God. Israel is the apple of God's eye.

"For thus says the LORD of hosts, "After glory He has sent me against the nations which plunder you, for he who touches you, touches the apple of His eye." Zechariah 2:8

God tells us in the Bible that He chose us, not the other way around, it has nothing to do with us. We did not have to be good enough, rather God chose us.

"You did not chose me, but I chose you and appointed you so that you might go and bear fruit--fruit that will last--and so that whatever you ask in my name the Father will give you." John 15:16

In the Old Testament, God chose leaders, disciples, prophets from all walks of life, to set before others as an example, often an example of good and bad.

The twelve disciples were not chosen because they were special, they were special because Jesus chose them. It is the same for you and me: we are not special; we are special because God chose us and adopted us to be His children.

Any jealousy other people or countries have about Israel being God's chosen people is actually ridiculous because the Jewish people never wanted to be chosen; but they were, and they have lived their lives trying to do life God's way.

They are huge humanitarians; they are usually one of the first countries to arrive with aid in the world when there is a crisis. They care for the poor and homeless, they care about the orphans and widows because God cares about them. Israel is such a generous nation.

The tension all started back in the Old Testament. Jewish, Christian and Muslim religions all trace their heritage back to Abraham. Abraham had 2 sons: Ishmael and Issac.

It started because people decided to "help God out". Abraham and Sarah were promised by God that they would have a son. Years passed and their bodies were way past child bearing days, even though it was a God promise, they waited, and waited, and when it did not happen Sarah convinced Abraham to sleep with her maid, Hagar, and have a son that way. When Hagar does get pregnant, Sarah, in jealousy, mistreats her and sends Hagar away. God sees and hears Hagar out in the desert and tells her to go back and that He will indeed bless her son and make him into a great nation.

Hagar names God as the "God who sees me." Genesis 6:13 She was able to deliver a son, Ismael.

"I will increase your descendants so much that they will be too numerous to count" Genesis 16:9

> *"You shall name him Ishmael [meaning "God hears"], for the Lord has heard of your misery. He will be a wild donkey of a man; his hand will be against everyone and everyone's hand against him, and he will live in hostility toward all his brothers" .Genesis 16:11–12*

Ishmael was born the natural way, the human way through a childbearing mother.

Fourteen years later, God came through as He always does, right on time to His way of thinking and Sarah did have a child, a son, they named him Isaac. Isaac was born supernaturally to parents who could no longer have children, a miracle baby.

God's Plan A – the Supernatural God way, was to supernaturally, give Abraham and Sarah a son, and to make that son, Isaac, into a great nation, a nation He called "His", the Jewish nation.

Abraham and Sarah chose instead to invest in Plan B with Ishmael, later when Sarah saw that she had a son herself, and Ishmael mocked her son, she mistreated Ishmael and his mother and sent them away again. Genesis 21:10

It is here, in this disrupted family of Abraham, Sarah, and Hagar where rejection, hurt and anger crept in. The hostility would continue between the Jews, Christians, Muslim nations to this day.

Ishmael would have 12 sons and the 12 Tribes of Ishmael were born.

Isaac had Jacob, who God changed his name to Israel had 12 sons and the 12 Tribes of Israel were born.

The Quran and the Bible separate at this point, but both make claims on Abraham. The Quran culminates in the prophet Mohammed while the Bible in the Christian faith culminates in the Son, Jesus.

All the hatred and heartache between the Arabs and the Israelites started as a result of God choosing to make a people that He would call, His. He would do it His way and only His way. The fact that people got in the middle and tried to help God, has muddied the waters to this very day.

Just like in the garden of Eden, humans decided they knew a better way and took the forbidden fruit and ate it. They too chose Plan B in their Plan A world, and we have been messed up ever since.

In our modern end day times, the end of time clock has 2 hands on it, the large hand is tick tocking its way around regarding the worlds timetable. The smaller hand represents the timetable of Israel. The smaller hand of Israel is nearing midnight, but the world hand still has some to go.

The fact that Israel has its own hand on the clock is a reason that makes the significance of this tiny country everyone's concern. God will only do His Plan A in our Plan B, C, D world. People will continue to try to change the plan, but in the end ONLY God's plan will prevail.

God has shown up over and over in the country of Israel even before it was the country of Israel. Jesus came to earth born in Bethlehem and then ending His life in Jerusalem. The angels who were with the disciples watching Jesus ascend to heaven said, *"He will come back just like you saw Him."* Acts 1:11

Jesus intends to come back to Jerusalem, that in its own right, makes Israel noticeable in the world scheme of things.

One of the things that made me giggle on my trip to Israel was when they took us by the eastern gate of the temple where Jesus is supposed to come back through.

In the Plan B world plan: that gate is now sealed shut, permanently and there are grave tombs scattered all around it. Those in the Muslim faith think that they have sealed the gate shut to prevent Jesus from entering and they have put unclean dead bodies in the way of the gate. Jewish people cannot touch dead bodies according to Jewish law. They think that because they have done these two things, Jesus will be stopped, but this is of course, just in case He really is real.

The giggle comes because I do not think they heard the stories of Jesus walking through walls, walking on the water, or even floating up to heaven. No gate or bodies will stop our resurrected Jesus when He decides it is time to return because it has always been God's Plan A and He will not be stopped.

Notes & Nuggets:

Notes & Nuggets:

About the Author:

Jane Wheeler lives in the oil town of Grande Prairie, Northern Alberta, Canada. Jane has three grown sons that bring joy, excitement and sometimes lots of prayer to her life.

Together with her husband they create amazing wood furniture and other treasures in their little woodshop.

God sees Jane as a teacher, leader, writer and builder. When she is physically not building in the woodshop, you will find her building into the Kingdom by teaching, leading and writing as God leads and directs her.

You can connect with her on her website where you will find her contact page, and a link to her weekly Wednesday Blog: *Midweek Moments* plus a list of other resources she has available.

If you wish to sign up to get her weekly blog emailed to you – please send a note on the contact page.

Website: http://www.rayofsunshineministries.com

www.ingramcontent.com/pod-product-compliance
Lightning Source LLC
LaVergne TN
LVHW051643080426
835511LV00016B/2461